CRITICAL ACCLAIM FOR *WARPATH*

"Form or fucking function? How about both? When so many PI novels are all about pretty form, damned few writers get the gritty function of real PI novels. Chandler, Hammett, Crais, Crumley. Those guys are the shit. So is Sayles. *Warpath* immerses you in his world, shows you what you'd rather not see, makes you hear his music his way. When Bruckner bleeds, we do, too. But it's not just pretty red, it means something, we learn from it. Read him...period."

—Trey R. Barker, author of
Death is Forever and *Slow Bleed*

"Buckner's back. More bloody, more bawdy, more biting...and more brutal. Sayles' wise-cracking, sardonic detective takes you along in the front seat for a ride on noir's wild side. Funny, dark and twisted. *Warpath* chafes against the cookie-cutter mysteries of yesteryear and serves up crime like no other. Not since Philip K. Dick has a writer created a narcotic so insidious as the Big Fry."

—Tom Pitts, author of
Knuckball and *Hustle*

"Buckner isn't nuts or a psychopath; he's just tired of all the bullshit that goes on in the game between criminals and cops and intelligently, he simply takes the most logical course of action in eradicating the animals who dare to breathe in his world. That he's the baddest bad ass in the neighborhood doesn't hurt. This is a ground-breaking book in just about every sense of the word. Sayles is a mighty talent and we're lucky to have him."

—Les Edgerton, author of *The Bitch, The Rapist, The Genuine, Imitation, Plastic Kidnapping* and others

"Richard Dean Buckner is a tough ex-police detective turned tougher private eye with at least .44 reasons not to call him Dick. Ryan Sayles pulls out all the stops as he races his protagonist along a frantic and treacherous *Warpath*."

—J.L. Abramo, award-winning author of *Gravesend, Brooklyn Justice* and others

WARPATH

BOOKS BY RYAN SAYLES

Richard Dean Buckner Mysteries
The Subtle Art of Brutality
Warpath
Albatross

Novels
Goldfinches
Together They Were Crimson
It's Ugly Because It's Personal
Like Whitewashed Tombs

Other Works
That Escalated Quickly!
I'm Not Happy 'til You're Not Happy
Let Me Put My Stories In You

Splits
C'mon and Do the Apocalypse with Brian Panowich
Two Bullets Solve Everything with Chris Rhatigan
Damn the Dark, Damn the Light with Grant Jerkins

RYAN SAYLES

WARPATH

A RICHARD DEAN BUCKNER MYSTERY

Crimson Gate Books

To my wife, for whom I do anything
and everything worthwhile.

To Brian P., who knew better than I did about this book.

To Eric C., who couldn't have been more generous.

To Zelmer Pulp, because.

1

Dusk, Sunday

He drops what has to be at least ten grand in front of me.

"I hope that's enough for you to at least listen," he says.

"It is." I take it and set it in my lap under the desk. Next to my .44 Magnum. For ten grand I'll listen to a drill bit shoved up someone's ass. Even if, at the end of our conversation I look this cat in the eye and tell him I'm not for hire, I'm keeping his money.

"I want you to work for me," he says. "Word has it you're, uhhh...*good* at what you do." He runs the back of his hand across his upper lip. Wipes away sweat beads collected in his mustache. In this setting, under these circumstances, that sweat can only mean one thing.

"I'm a private detective," I say. "Not an assassin."

"Come again?"

"If you want someone found, I'll find him." I lean in, smoke curling from my nostrils. Dragon. "If you want someone murdered, take a fucking hike." Looming, I jab a thumb at the office door.

"No, no, no. I want someone found. That's all. *Found*," he says. More sweat beads. No eye contact. Fidgeting.

He wants someone murdered.

Clarence T. Petticoat. Fifties, tan and lean. Well dressed. Pretty. It is obvious by his appearance that his appearance matters. He's a real estate giant in the city. I know he handles residential stuff—mostly top dollar cookie-cutter mini-mansions—but his real gig? Commercial. Looking at this guy, it makes sense.

The scene: my office. Last week of March. Spring has come in weak doses but it's getting a little stronger every day. The last hour of daylight bleeds through my picture window and fights a losing battle to illuminate the room through the veil of cigarette smoke and dust.

Petticoat looks nervous like he's a middle schooler buying pot for the first time. A man this successful in a business where one must be equal parts smooth, charming and ruthless doesn't become this flaccid in front of strangers. Whether he considers it this way or not, he wants me to be his employee if not a business partner. He's quaking and jabbering over a twenty-year-old wound like it happened yesterday. He's good. I'll give him that. He's got the whole broken man act going on and half of it is grade A horseshit. I'll stake that the pain is at least based on a kernel of truth.

The best lies are.

I adjust in my seat and eyeball him. "I've seen your type. And, on a side note, I've arrested most of them for kiddie porn, but that's neither here nor there. Mr. Petticoat, you offer me ten big ones 'just to listen.' All the sweat. All the nerves. The way you checked the street when you walked up to the building. The way you scanned the hall as you came to my office. Even from my window I can see plain as day you drove a rental here. You're a shrewd business man and *word has it* you're as cutthroat as they come in high-stakes real estate. So cut the shit. You're nervous about something and it ain't *finding someone*."

"I know how this looks," he says. Clears his throat. "I just want someone found."

"Of course. Sure you do. Who then?" I ask.

"I don't know his name. All I know is he killed my wife."

I raise an eyebrow and Petticoat immediately babbles, "Well—I guess I should say, er—what I mean is, he *led to the death* of my wife. That's more accurate."

I keep the eyebrow up. "Led to her death? Did he kill her?"

"She killed herself."

"Did he sell her dope and she OD'd on it?"

"No. They never met like that."

"What then?"

His mouth trembles, eyes fight tears. Sounds escape around his tight lips like cries for help working around a gag.

"Affair?" I ask. "She was going to leave you for this guy, and as it turns out he wouldn't leave his wife for her? And your wife couldn't bear it?"

Shakes his head. "I said they never met like that."

I sit back. For a business mogul this guy is as tender as a bitch in heat. Of course we're talking about his dead bride here. I open my desk drawer and pull out a bottle of whiskey. Drop it on the table with a *thud* loud enough to make him jump in his seat.

I keep a sleeve of plastic cups for guests. I pour him a shot.

"Bottom's up," I say and I sound like my old man. I push him the cup.

"I don't drink," he manages to say around a lump in his throat.

"Then do whatever it is you do to pull yourself together and get on with this." I shoot the swill myself. Good sting. It rises up through my face and gives the kind of internal swat that you want in an eye-opener.

"I should start by saying I'm having an operation in eight days—"

"Start by saying who you want found," I say. Pour another shot.

Deep breath. Shudder. Begins. "In 1992 my wife and I came home from the movies. We walked into our house during an invasion."

I settle in for a narrative. It's no use; he'll begin where he thinks the story begins. One hand in my lap next to the comforting weight of the ten grand and the even more comforting weight of the revolver. My left hand rolling the plastic cup around in my palm like it was a meditation exercise.

"I was struck right away—" He reaches a hand up to the crown of his skull; a ghost motion he probably doesn't know he does every time he recounts this story. "—she was, *assaulted*. I think it was only one man. Her rape kit only revealed one, ummm...*intruder*."

"DNA?" DNA was a fledgling thing in the SAPD back in the early '90s. It was still considered voodoo by some in law enforcement. It probably won't matter.

"None," he says, looking down at his hands. "There was a lubricant commonly associated with some brand of condoms. No semen. Sheila—my wife—she described one man. Said he was behind the door. My mom always said I was so rude. I—"

He stops. Looks away to his happy place. One way to get a witness to recall a crime is to have them close their eyes and re-imagine the whole thing. Pull that skin back on for a minute, like a snake sliding inside its shed husk to recall the taste of the last mouse it ate while in it.

When interviewing a witness to a gas station robbery, have them sit there and imagine pulling into the parking space. Mime putting the gear shift in park. Turn off the engine. Hot outside? Stuffy inside the car? What side of the vehicle was the sunlight coming in? Now, when the first robber ran out the door, which way did he turn?

This is how it goes. Petticoat here, he's remembering the worst night of his life. Tugging back on that shed skin.

"It's funny," he starts up. "I always opened a door and walked through it first. My mom said it was the rudest thing. I remember on prom night I did that and she jumped my ass right there in front of my date. I was so proud of myself later because for the rest of the night I let my date through first. But as soon as the night was over, I just reverted. I went back to walking through a door first."

"Did he take anything? Did he burglarize the home? Did he remove any property?"

"No. He just waited."

"Did he take a trophy from your wife? A memento of the rape?"

"Yes. Her panties."

Some rapists, along with other douche bags like serial killers and Ronald McDonald, they'll take something by which to remember the occasion when they are finished with the crime. They'll stash it and look at it occasionally to relive the thrill of the event. Lockets, jewelry, a trinket, a clip of hair, clothing, a photograph, a body part. Developing a suspect and then raiding the suspect's house has led to the discovery of a treasure trove of these mementos. It helps police connect one suspect to dozens of crimes.

"Who did the police suspect?"

"Nobody. They might as well not have worked the case."

"How so?"

"There was nothing to go on," Petticoat says, closer to a whine. "No prints. Neighbors didn't see anything. No DNA. The attacker didn't speak. Wore a mask. After he clubbed me, Sheila was already stepping inside. He bashed her in the face. He duct taped her hands behind her back. She couldn't scrape him. No skin under her nails. Nothing."

He stares at my desk like it is the very grave of his wife. "They had nothing to go on."

"Who worked the case?"

"A guy named Gillispie. Trevor Gillispie. I'll never forget that name. It was the only one I got through the whole ordeal."

Trevor Gillispie was a pretty good detective when it came to property crimes. He transferred to sex crimes and failed miserably. Of course, about that time the rumor was that his wife caught him with another man. Gillispie stayed on the job through his separation and ugly divorce. Then, about a year later he ate his gun. He'll be no help now.

"So," I say and shoot the whiskey. "Let me speed this up. Gillispie doesn't turn up anything. Eventually the case goes cold."

"Yes."

"You get the famous Saint Ansgar Victim Letter where you're told the case is being closed but will be reopened as soon as any new developments arise."

"Yes."

The SAPD had reams of those things, preprinted and just waiting to be rubberstamped with a signature and mailed. Box after box of form letters waiting to be the last domino in someone's horrible chain of events.

"And your wife, in her despair, commits suicide," I say this, aware of how cold it sounds. I suppose I could have said *took her own life, fell to her own hand, ended her suffering* or some bullshit along those lines. Sugar-coating a decision never did anyone any good.

"She, uhhh...Sheila couldn't come out of her suffering. She was so damn despondent. And I was no help," Petticoat says. If everything he's said is true up to this point, he was lying there next to her unconscious the entire time her life was being systematically dismantled. When a man vows before God to love, cherish, honor, protect, blah blah blah and then he doesn't do it when it matters most, I can see the torture. The guilt.

"So in the end Sheila...she ended her suffering."

Ahhh. Good choice of words, Petticoat. I light a new smoke. "And now you want me to find the rapist?"

"Yes."

"And then hand him over to the police?" Here comes the assassin part.

"Of course," Petticoat says, as if the raging need to cause this criminal tenfold the agony he has suffered doesn't factor in to our deal at all.

Petticoat shrugs and looks away with some empty amusement and huffs out with a dry laugh. "Well, *maybe* he can fall down once or twice as you're walking him up the steps to headquarters."

I sit back, watching as he places his hands on the steering wheel of our conversation and starts a gradual but irrevocable turn.

A change of tone as clear as the difference between life and death. "You'll get another ten grand if you accept me as a client."

Petticoat opens his blazer and I see four more stacks of bills inside a pocket. He's done them up very deliberately. Show off. He wants to appeal to my fiscal side.

"Twenty more upon delivery."

"Delivery? Or conviction?"

"Delivery."

I give him a skeptical eye. "This is a great deal for me, Mr. Petticoat."

He nods. He knows business. This is *too* great for me.

"It makes me suspicious."

"Why? You don't have bills to pay?"

"Money is money. If I'm that strapped for cash I can just walk down the street and find a drug dealer to shake down." I crush out my smoke and steeple my fingers in front of me, elbows on the desk. "You don't get the street reputation I have for being gentle with the scum of the earth. So let me lay this out for you."

"Please do, Mr. Buckner. I'm getting the feeling you think I'm trying to take a dishonest angle with you."

"Dishonest? Maybe. Suspicious? Abso-fucking-lutely."

"I see."

I light a new smoke. "A guy rolls into your house, commits at least four felonies that I can pick out from your statement right now. The PD gets nowhere. More than twenty years go by and you want to meet. You very deliberately want it to be dusk because dawn and dusk are the two hardest light conditions to see under. Ask any driver staring into a low-lying sun who gets into a wreck. You rent a car, you wear sunglasses, a hat, a high collar and I see you've grown a goatee. Your ads on the bus benches and your TV commercials have you clean-shaven. You passed by three times before you parked down the street. Bottom line: you don't want witnesses."

"I'm careful," he says. "I lead a public life. All I need is someone seeing me speaking with a private detective and they'll think I am digging around against one of my competitors. I have seven-figure deals on the table right now, Mr. Buckner. I—"

"I don't care," I say. "Like you give a shit about your competitors." I know for a fact that Howard Michigan has done just that kind of work for Petticoat here. His veil is thinning as we speak.

"You drop money in my lap to 'listen' and then you show off a bunch more. You're very deliberate in the sums you offer, and after what you've shown me inside your jacket, there's still some wads that have not been accounted for. I'm assuming I get to empty your pockets if I show up with a man who...took some time dying."

"You said you're not an assassin."

"I did. But I'm sure you're thinking to yourself it won't hurt to ask."

"I brought the money to negotiate with. That's all. You don't advertise your fees."

"Oh. Boy Scout. I see."

"Business."

"You'll pay on delivery."

"Yes."

"So what's to stop me from just looking up a known rapist, beating him into a coma and dropping him on your front door? Will you take anybody? Is your thirst for revenge that blind?"

"You're reputation bars against that, Mr. Buckner. I have

full faith you'll solve this—"

"So tell me, Mr. Petticoat, I have just one question."

"Is it, *where do I sign?*"

"No. How do you expect me to get anywhere further than Gillispie did back when the crime was still hot? Why even bother now?"

He rubs his face. His hands shake. "Mr. Buckner, that's *two* questions."

"Don't correct me."

"I'm sorry. I'm just so...so damn *tired.* Like I said I'm having an operation next week—"

"Like *I* said—" Bored with this game now. "—cut the shit."

He huffs long and exhausted. His eyes dart about. I note his pupils, even in this dim light, are pinpoints. A tell.

"You'll succeed where the police failed because I...I have information I—" He looks down and balls a fist. Holds it to his mouth. He mumbles something like *forgive me Sheila* as his eyes quake with guilt.

Very small, as if the utterance of these words is enough to tear silk: "I have information I did not give them."

The room is still. Even the ghosts I have made throughout my life who cling to me now stop their haunting and lean in closer.

"What information?" I ask.

"The rapist's girlfriend. I know who she is."

2

"You held back that kind of information?"

"Yes. Don't think it doesn't eat me up inside."

I study him for a second and guess what? I don't see him eaten at all. Something that egregious would leave all kinds of gnawing marks. Chunks torn out and still bloody after all these years. But strangely, he looks calm, like he's a few steps into a choreographed rant now. A tell. "Why?"

He inhales in a very practiced manner. "The way it came about...it's a long story."

"Did you have it at the time?"

He covers his mouth. He says too loudly, "No." Tells. This is getting thick.

"Well, Mr. Petticoat. Maybe I can help you," I say, easing back my chair.

A brilliant, relief-soaked smile. "I knew it! I knew it! I've got the best man in this line of work on my side now and—"

I stand. Slide the packet of bills into my suit coat pocket. Forty-four Magnum in hand. I don't point it at him. Not yet.

"Get out," I say, as unwavering as if he were a bar fly I'd picked up and brought her home just to discover she has a boner. In both situations, I don't play these games.

"Now, Mr. Buckner." Instead of leaving he slinks down into the small chair I have for guests and crosses a leg rather effeminately. He draws his head down between his shoulders as if he's a turtle getting ready for decapitation.

One hand to the side of his face and he says, "Mr. Buckner there is no reason why we can't—"

"I suggest you go to the police. Tell them about this girlfriend and they can connect the dots from there."

I cock the hammer back on the revolver and his face freezes into wide eyes and granite. "But, Mr. Petticoat, you're so full of shit that *I'm* done listening. So, *get out.*"

He holds his hands out to me, palms up. He won't make eye contact. He very slowly reaches into the pocket of his jacket and withdraws another packet of money. A flick of his wrist and it lands with a *thud* onto my desk.

"So the last ten grand had run out of listening time. Okay. Sure," he says, lowering his hands slowly like he was underwater. "Just let me buy some more time. Okay? Okay?"

Twenty grand?

Twenty grand.

"Fine." The .44 goes away. I sit down, take the packet of bills and flutter them with my thumb, looking to make sure each one has ol' Benjamin on it. Satisfied, the packet goes inside my jacket next to the other one.

"The girlfriend. Why me instead of the police. Your real intentions. Get this over with."

"Right, right," he says, wiping away more sweat. "The girlfriend's name is Carla Gabler. Well, I should say ex-girlfriend. And let me clarify: *I* did not have the information at the time. My buddy, he got it later."

Double-back. A tell.

"What buddy?"

"Dan Martins. He was a parole officer with the city. Gabler, she was at Happenstance prison up north. You know, the women's prison? Anyway, she was in for robbing houses I think, and when she got out, Dan was her PO."

He rubs the bridge of his nose. "Actually, Dan says he had been making house calls with her as well."

Parole officer shitting where he eats. Sounds like a quality guy.

"Dan said one night during some pillow talk, she was recounting her life. Telling him about the boyfriend she used to date who got her in trouble. She went with him and they robbed a house and they got busted. That's how she got imprisoned. She said his name, but Dan never told me. Then she said something about him robbing *my* house. I guess he had just gotten out as well, I don't know."

Petticoat's face is forlorn. His fists bunch up, his shoulders tighten. "Carla Gabler."

"Dan didn't say anything because he didn't make the connection? Or was he too shitty to mention *how* he got the info because he didn't want to lose his job?" I ask, light a smoke.

"Dan never said." Petticoat's voice is flat as ash. "But I know Dan. I know that guy. He just didn't want to lose his job."

"When did he tell you?"

"Right after his retirement party." Petticoat's eyes sternly examine the floor in front of him. "Last month."

I write down the names.

Deep breath, then he says, "My real intensions." He laughs, hollow. Like a smoker who should have quit long ago but still lights a cancer stick around his oxygen tank. Petticoat's merriment sounds like old paper being torn.

"Another buddy of mine sent me to you. Hank Madison. He said you were the kind of guy who could walk into maximum security in the prison and those felons would step back. He said you've been off the force long enough for the new policemen to not know who you are, but for some reason, criminals who started yesterday *do* know you. Like you're a chapter in their *How to Commit Crimes* handbook. The "Don't Fuck With This Guy" chapter. Hank said you've earned that reputation."

Hank Madison is an old friend of mine from the force. He and I were never so close that we exchanged Christmas presents, I've never met his wife, but we are cool. It's been a long time. I make a note to buy Madison a round. Nothing warms my heart like people telling other people I am the baddest motherfucker of all-time.

"I figure a reputation like that gets earned with a solid punch here and there. So sure, I figured once you got your hands on the rapist you'd pop him one for me. But I'm not hiring you to kill him. I'm not. I just...want him."

"Okay," I say.

"And why *you* rather than the police? Well, for starters they have already failed me once. Second, you're a dedicated asset. If I drop cash in front of a Saint Ansgar detective and say 'make this your only case,' it's a bribe. A defense lawyer can use that to get the rapist off. But, if I do that to you, it's a fee. And, as I've said, I have an operation coming up in eight days."

Here's the twist among the rest of his questionable story.

"Heart problems. The cardiac surgeon says if I get the surgery, my chances of survival are thirty-five to forty percent. If I do not, I'll be dead within six months. Bottom line. Don't get me wrong; I think the university hospital is great an all—especially for cardiac stuff—but c'mon."

He holds both hands palms up, adjusting them in the air like they are weight scales. "Die on a table in a hospital, surrounded by doctors and nurses and medicine while I'm under anesthesia, or die at home, doped up on morphine, having severe heart arrhythmias and needing a defibrillator hooked up to me all the time?"

He puts his hands down. Looks right at me, more direct that any other time this evening. "I'm sure a man of your ilk wants to die in a glorious battle with swords and cannon fire and all that jazz, but a man like me, who has money-making deals on the table right now, he wants to die a long time from now, Mr. Buckner. A *long time*."

"Sure."

"So, I want you as opposed to PD because I need this case reopened and solved in eight days. I want to know the man who raped my wife and destroyed everything I ever had has been caught before I wager sixty to sixty-five percent odds I'll never wake up."

He leans in. Like a multi-million dollar real estate transaction with the final word hanging out in space, waiting to be said, he gets a confident look that I imagine he has as he shakes hands and walks away that much richer.

"Mr. Buckner, do we have a deal?"

"You said twenty grand more just to take the case?"

"Yes."

"You said you just want someone delivered?"

"Yes."

"You said there's a good chance you might be dead in eight days?"

"Yes."

"Sure, we have a deal," I say. "Why the hell not?"

3

Evening, Sunday

The two biggest factors that solve cold cases are DNA and new testimony from witnesses.

Sometimes a witness will see the entire crime unfold before his eyes and be too afraid to ever speak up. The police might identify said witness as what he is: the most important thing to solve the crime. But the witness doesn't want to get involved. So he shuts up. And the perp walks.

Then, years later, the perp dies or gets incarcerated. Gets shot during another crime, becomes a victim himself, gets locked up on another charge and will never get out. Then, the witness grows a pair and comes forward with his story. And the perp gets prosecuted on an old crime.

That solves cold cases.

DNA. Same thing. It was developed in the early '80s in England and used as a profiling technique. The process filtered across the rest of the world and eventually found its way into the United States' court system where it has damned many guilty parties and exonerated those few people in prison who weren't lying when they said they were innocent.

Petticoat left his copy of the case report he was given by Detective Gillispie all those years ago. The bulk of it is the offense report where Gillispie spells out in very finite detail the events of the night. There are also statements from the Petticoats themselves, reproductions of crime scene photographs, what the rape kit found, et cetera.

The best bet is to call in a favor at the PD and have the rapist's DNA sampled from the original evidence stilled being stored in records and sent to an independent lab where they can test it against all the DNA on file with the Department of Corrections. Hopefully our rapist was imprisoned for something, *anything*, and the guy can get tagged with this as well. The problem will be the timeframe. I know a lab that works very fast for the right dollar amount, but I'll need to push a lot at the PD to get the paperwork through and approved in time.

Then of course, there's the other problem. Petticoat is lying about something.

There is ample proof that what he said happened did actually happen. He has the lofty position in life to legitimately pay me the sums he has shelled out. I can understand the fear, the revenge. I'm widowed as well but I can't readily find cancer and beat it to death. Petticoat has it easier than that.

There's something up his sleeve. Before this is over with I'll have him take his shirt off. At gun point, if need be.

I call Howard Michigan.

Howard, what passed for a training officer on the PD back when I started, he's been a private eye for years now. Numerous alimony payments dictate he do something. Howard mostly follows around the wives of rich men and reports back, or he staples missing person flyers up and down the streets on light posts and billboards.

Howard is horrible at almost everything he does except making things harder on himself. The man excels at two other things: smoking unfiltered cigarettes and falling in love with women who will one day divorce him in very ugly terms. But, on the other hand he knows just about everybody. He's the guy that knows a guy who can do or get just about whatever it is you need.

He answers on the second ring. "Hello?"

"Howard, Richard."

"Hey! Richard. You gotta come by some time. I got my hands on some good scotch. *Good* scotch."

"Sure." Sounds like he's working his way through it right now. "You know Clarence Petticoat?"

"Petticoat?" Groans while he searches his dusty memory. "The real estate guy? Or the black dwarf who used to work at that retirement home and went to prison for thieving from the old biddies who would die in their sleep?"

"Black dwarf? What are you talking about? Clarence Petticoat, the real estate guy. You've done work for him."

"Oh, right, right. Never mind about the dwarf guy. That might have been a movie I seen."

"Are you sober?"

"I can be. What's the gig?"

"No gig. I wanted to ask you about this guy. He hired me to find the man who raped his wife back in '92."

"No gig? Fine. I'm drunk. Petticoat's wife was raped? How bad?"

That's no shit. In Howard's mind there is a sliding scale of sexual assault. On the low end there is the woman who had consensual sex with someone and later decided her palette was indeed too discerning for her experience with such a panty-sniffer to be anything but rape. On the high end there is Petticoat's wife; the woman blindsided by a "true" rapist, battered, hospitalized, et cetera.

"Aggravated rape, aggravated battery. During an aggravated burglary. Later she killed herself."

"Okay. So it was *rape* rape."

"Yes, Howard."

"Funny. He never mentioned it."

"Do all the clients who hire you to do a background check on the pool boy before they leave them at home with the trophy wife tell you about aggravated felonies? The police called it a *rape* rape. Petticoat gave me the case file," I say, flipping through the pages, looking at nothing in particular. "Gillispie worked it. Poorly, I might add."

"Gillispie, Gillispie..." Howard trails off and I can hear the ice in a glass clinking around as he takes a swallow from whatever is going to cause his hangover in the morning. "I remember a guy named Gillispie who died in a high-speed car chase."

"Not him. You're thinking of Ginsbee. Sam Ginsbee. I'm talking about Thomas Gillispie. Property crimes."

"Oh. *Oh!* The dead queen. Why did they send a burglary dick to work a rape?"

"I don't know, Howard. Who fucking cares? What can you tell me about Petticoat?"

"White guy. Successful. Tall. Very pretty."

On a side note, if I were Petticoat, it would drive me nuts that heterosexual men describe me as pretty. I also despise talking to Howard when he's drunk, which is more and more these days. He thinks his drunken, sophomoric humor stops even the most stiff-legged individual in his tracks and sends him into fits of roaring laughter. It's amusing enough when I don't need something. When I do, I can barely stop myself from slugging him in the solar plexus to get him to vomit up all that expensive booze. I immediately start thinking of ways to put the hurt to him.

I crush out my smoke as hard as I want to smash Howard. "Are you going to get your head out of your ass and answer my question or do I need to call you tomorrow morning at seven a.m.?"

He gives me a *ha* that sounds more like a raspy *huff:* "You know I don't wake up until one p.m. or so, Richard. I won't answer."

"You know I'll let it ring until you get up to disconnect the line."

"You know I'll just do that tonight before I go to bed."

"You know you'll forget as soon as we hang up."

"You know—damn it, Richard. Don't call that early. I get the worst fucking migraine when I wake up hung over that early."

"Answer my question then."

"Yes!" he shouts, superbly annoyed. "Yes, I remember Gillispie!"

"*That's* not the question."

"Yes, it was!"

"I asked—" A tone chirps in my ear. Graham Clevenger beeps in. "I've got to go, Howard. I'm calling you tomorrow at seven. No. Make that five."

"Richard! You fu—"

I click over.

Howard Michigan was the first generation of hard-drinking, hard-fighting cop on the force. I was the second. The difference between Howard and I is that Howard was a terrible cop and I was good. When I was labeled as *unfit for service,* excused and "allowed to medically retire," I had been partnered with the third generation of cop. Graham Clevenger. He didn't drink hard. He fought hard, but never "went overboard" like Howard and I were always accused of. Graham was simply a professional. We are not partners anymore, nor have we been for some time. But if I were to consider the words *best friend,* or really, *only friend,* Graham Clevenger gets the title.

"Evening, Graham. Thanks for getting me off the phone with Howard Michigan."

"Sure, Richard," he says. Sounds tired. I'm rubbing my eyes from the frustration with my old trainer. Now I have to get up early to call him and send his entire day into a flaming tailspin just out of spite.

I ask, "Ever heard of a guy named Clarence Petticoat? Real estate monster here in town?"

"Yes."

"He's backed the money truck up to my front door so I'll find a rapist from the early '90s. I might need your help getting some DNA out of the records unit. Do you mind?"

"I'll be off work for a few days," he is slow to say. "I'll actually be needing your assistance..."

"Off work? Why? Painting your house?"

"No."

I do a double take at the clock. Almost 2300 hours. Clevenger doesn't call this late for shits and giggles.

"Graham, what's wrong?" I ask, instinctively shrugging on my jacket.

"I need you to meet me at 3917 Bending Boulevard. North end of the city. Now."

"On my way. I assume this is about giving someone some help."

Giving someone some help is our code phrase for fucking up someone. If a man can't stop himself from beating his kids, I consider it help to break that man's back. It's harder to punch a child when you have to lean over a wheelchair to do it.

"Yes."

"Tell me what happened, Graham."

"Gang. Drive-by...they hit the wrong house," Clevenger says. His voice is coming from a desert somewhere far away where shattered men go when they've lost their way. "They killed Grandma."

4

In the days following the hit attempt that left me with a damaged brain and no job, Clevenger was there.

In the days following the drug case that hammered coffin nails into six drug peddlers and hammered a revenge-needle into my neck, Clevenger was there.

In the days following me coming to in a hospital, delirious and confused, enraged and swimming in the after-effects of a designer drug that did more killing than drugging, Clevenger was there.

My old partner in the homicide bureau, the detective who took my place as reigning king, the only man who is my family now.

As a homicide detective I got my ass in deep trouble. Rather than fire me I was transferred away from Graham and into Living Hell: stolen autos. To get any action I started volunteering for undercover buys on a big bust against a drug cooked up by Satan himself. Called *The Big Fry*, it was cheap and lethal. The first dose killed some users outright, let others live just to rot them out slowly. But with some it caused what we coined as *Gray Matter Detonation*, which was a fancy term for becoming a vegetable. Imagine a bunker-buster of a stroke with permanent bloodshot eyes, drooling lips and absolutely nothing else. No response to stimulus. Confined to diapers and IV diets. Damnation this side of hell.

And then there was another group, small. Handpicked by Fate herself to suck it slowly. The smeared. They have a bizarre brain chemical reaction that foils the drug's ability to kill instantly. Instead, like acid flashbacks, the drug pops back up here and there. Just in bursts. Smears.

I helped another detective named Garrett take down some folks associated with Big Fry, and their associates found me one day and shot me up with a lethal dose. Left me for dead. I found a hospital before death found me. But the dose wrecked my brain before giving up. I'm smeared.

So imagine me in some recovery ward, in and out of consciousness for days. Nearly sixty, still built like a bull surrounded by all those nurses, having what they called "an episode." Disassociation from reality.

Me snapping out of it, wrapping the lines and wires around my fists like chain around a street boxer's knuckles, yanking. Flying off whatever tenuous handle medical staff had established for me. Wanting to make sense of it, wanting revenge of my own, wanting to beat and claw and destroy my way back to a frame of mind that wasn't composed of threads and flashbacks.

The smears like waterfalls of boiling oil colored like rainbows, each one washing ice over my mind. That consuming needle of brain-freeze stabbing down my neck, radiating a sensation close to death but too much of a cocktease to really be it. Red to orange to brown to purple to blue to black to unconsciousness. I couldn't handle it. It was like filling a turkey baster with liquid agony and shooting it behind my eyes.

I'd go apeshit in that room. Storm the hall, gown flapping in the wind and blood pouring down my arms from the IVs I had just torn out and flung across the room. Shameful. But if I could kill a mountain of people to regain what that single injection had taken from me, in those moments, Big Fry smears painting nightmares on the canvas of my *everything,* I would do it. I would kill until I had it back.

Clevenger was there. Other than him, I had no one. No one except Clevenger and his wife Molly. People with no reason to love me but who still did. Beyond partners, beyond boys in blue looking out for their own. We're family.

I know we brawled. Probably more than once. But despite whatever foul words I spouted, whatever taunts and chest-poking, Graham just cared for me enough to wrestle a destroyed and naked old man back into his bed. Pin him down until his episode passed. Until he finished disassociating from reality and came back to all those nice, clean associated people.

My captain never came to visit. The guys I worked beside, they never came. Garrett kind-of had an excuse because the same guys who hit me got their mitts on him. He lived. Barely.

It was just me, Clevenger and Molly, the incessant beeping of the monitoring equipment, the loving spirit of my dead wife who no doubt watched over me and all my nightmares in that damn hospital.

And I was there way too long.

5

Evening, Sunday

Saint Ansgar's finest are there when I arrive.

Night is heavier here than it was back at my place. The street lamps hum in tones of piss yellow and ill green up and down the street. Emergency lights spill LED red and blue in alternating punches along the homes. The bitter tinge to the air feels purposeful tonight; as if evening were a woman baring her teeth at what has occurred here.

Clevenger stands on the porch, running a hand through his hair. The brilliant red caresses him and he looks soaked in blood. The blue washes over and he looks like a phantom.

Behind him, the scene of the crime is really nothing more than an unassuming one-story ranch. The house faces east with a two-car driveway but only a one-car garage. A picture window, some decorative shutters and his grandma's flower garden. Looking at the garden, which is still a bare patch of earth waiting for warmer climates so it may be planted, like Graham. A bare patch of humanity, now. Just waiting.

I get out of the car, crush my smoke onto the concrete. A homicide detective walks about, speaking with a CSI tech. Another tech is busy placing numbered markers next to bullet holes in the house so he can take photographs. Other markers are scattered like a game of marbles in the street, each standing sentinel over a spent shell casing.

The difference between this homicide and all the others I've ever worked is Clevenger. Any other homicide and we'd be standing there, not reverent to the deceased but cautious that we do not disturb any damning evidence. Talking not about how the victim baked strawberry and rhubarb pies for him as a child but instead debating which burger joint had better onion rings or make jokes that would be considered callous or distasteful to those not accustomed to seeing death as a matter of course.

Graham sees me, nods. No smile. Instead his face hardens and I know what he wants at once. The PD won't let him near this one. Not in a million years. He'll have good people on it, but he wouldn't have asked me to come down here, be at the crime scene, if he didn't want me on it as well.

The weight of my revolver settles in against me. Nudging like a hound asking to be unleashed. Give it time. Those responsible will show themselves.

I look up and down the street. The powerful flash from the tech's camera bleaches my vision, even as it reaches over my shoulders to attack my eyes.

Flash. Frozen in time, two neighbors have actually taken a seat on their porch, mugs in hand.

Flash. Down the block, people in their robes, stand on the sidewalk at what they must believe a safe distance, curious as to the fatal outcome. Gawkers. I'm sure they were woken by the barrage of *pops* in the early night, and after they heard the wail and shriek of sirens they felt safe enough to come outside.

I turn towards the house again just as a uniform walks up to me.

Flash. He's young, twenty-four maybe. Tight haircut, neat uniform. Very presentable. "Detective Buckner?"

"Yes."

"Detective Clevenger asked me to escort you through, sir."

We walk past all the cop garbage, the crime scene tape, stepping around the CSI shit unpacked and piled. Past relics of the deceased; poured concrete statues of a garden gnome and a fawn. A small collection of blown glass decorations. All memories for Graham to avoid right now.

Flash. Clevenger's face has lost weight, added years and not slept in a decade all at once. His eyes glisten but do not run over. His lips won't move the way he wants them to. I've seen it before from the families of other victims. I hate applying that term to Clevenger but it's the hard truth. Clevenger pats me on the shoulder; he dare not say anything for a moment.

When interviewing victims beginning with yes or no questions is decent lubricant for the flow of speech. It avoids what might otherwise be difficult terrain.

"Molly stay at home?" I ask.

Nods.

"Been inside yet?"

Nods.

"News media arrived?"

Shakes his head. Good. Shootings are not new to our city and if the camera crews rolled out for every shot fired they'd be constantly running from one to the next. This might draw some vultures though. It's newsworthy when gangs get it so wrong. And when the victim is an elderly woman—a grandmother of a police detective no less—they'll smell blood in the water and want to report it.

Careful, now. "Anyone else inside? Your grandfather lives here as well, right?"

"Yes." Spoken delicately, trying to find his voice. "He went with her."

Clevenger sounds a fraction more unwavering with each word. He's a strong man. A deep breath or two and he'll be where I need him so we can get moving on this.

"Where did they go?"

"Anna Long Memorial."

"That's the best one." Anna Long Memorial hospital is well established in the area as the highest-quality hospital in a five hundred mile radius. It is all the things a hospital should be: clean, hopeful, well-staffed, caring and most of all, healing.

We both know his grandma died in her bed, but if the ambulance wants to cart her off to the hospital and have her pronounced there, so be it.

"Have you spoken with the detective yet?" I ask.

"No. He got here thirty seconds before you did."

"Is he good?"

"Yes. Name's DeMarcus Collins. I called the captain and said he's the one I want."

"Good for you." Calling a superior and telling them who *they're* going to assign to *your* case is ballsy. Clevenger learned a lot of ballsy by watching me, however, so it makes me proud for him to do it. With Clevenger being the head homicide detective he knows his men and should get who he wants.

"I'm going to have a chat," I say. I step down and walk out into the yard.

"Detective Collins?"

He looks up. The man is so black his features get lost in the chill evening. The cut of his face and neck belong to a stone statue. This man could be stomping down a fashion runway in New York City just as easily as arresting bad guys.

"Yes?"

"I'm Richard Dean Buckner. I know Detective Sergeant Clevenger. He asked me to come here."

"I've heard of you. He talks about you. So do the old timers at the bureau. Did you really shoot the mayor's son?"

Of course they still talk about it. If it were someone else's story, I know I'd still tell it.

"Yeah, I did." I light a smoke. "Back in '81."

"One day you'll have to tell me about it."

"One day." Not now.

We stand quiet for a moment. The lightning flash shot of levity from my story fades out as meaningless conversation during hard times does. "What have you got so far?"

He leafs through two pages of notes. Then: "No ID on the suspects or the vehicle. One neighbor said he was outside and heard the shots being fired but 'couldn't recall' a make, model or color of the car."

"They never can."

"Yes. Shots were fired around ten-fifteen. We count nine shell casings in the street. We've found twenty-eight holes in the house. Detective Clevenger's grandmother was struck twice, lying in bed."

"DRT?"

"Yes, sir."

DRT. Dead Right There. Collins' tone is respectful as he acknowledges her death; he knows I'm a friend of the family and more specifically a friend of his boss.

"What about his grandfather?"

"Untouched. Woke up, said it took a minute to figure out what just happened, then he called nine-one-one. We'd already gotten three calls before him. Already had units on the way."

"Are you going on the assumption that this drive-by was a fuck up? They got the wrong house?"

"Yes."

"Check the neighbors? Could it be they were one house off?"

"I'm getting to that, yeah. I've been looking up and down the street. Seeing if there is something that stands out. Anything that says *gangbanger lives here*. Could just be that some punk kid from south of the river was sent by his mom up here to live with grandma and grandpa and trouble followed him. There might be a drug house nestled in somewhere. I'll get as ridiculous as it takes to figure this out. Right now, if I see a pit bull, a low rider, anyone, *anyone* trotting around with sagging pants, that's my suspect. I'll just have to get him to talk."

Gears are turning. I take in what he says and it starts to come together for me. "You get many calls to this neighborhood? I've been out of the game long enough, maybe things have changed."

"How so?"

"When I was on the force this place was just like it seems now: a sleepy, older neighborhood. Have things changed?" I'm curious.

"No. Don't think so."

"Why the drive-by here at all?"

"Did Clevenger piss someone off? Maybe it's revenge." Collins is asking me, as if I'm his superior.

"Maybe," I say, not meaning it. I look back to Clevenger and my plan is in my mind, swirling. "I'll see you later, Collins. Do Graham proud."

"I will, Detective. It's an honor to meet you."

"Thanks." I walk back to Clevenger.

"What do you think?" he asks as I walk up.

"Good kid. He's got some ideas."

"Yeah. Is he digging in deep about the neighbors?"

"Yes, he is."

"My grandparents moved out here from Wyoming in the late sixties. They bought this house then. I remember visiting as a kid. It's also one of the reasons why I wanted to get stationed here. I know this neighborhood. There is no reasonable gang target on these streets."

"I agree."

"I don't want a trial, Richard."

"I'm sure you don't."

"My grandmother was a midwife for thirty years. My grandfather got the bronze star in World War Two. This is complete bullshit. This should have never happened."

"So you ask for the PD detective who is good, but whom you know to be narrowly focused?"

"Yes." Calculated.

"He'll make the investigation look good on paper. He'll put forth the honest effort to bring these punks to justice."

"Yes." Frank.

"And then you ask me to show up."

"Yes." Firm.

"So there won't be a trial."

"Yes." Cold.

I need you to meet me at 3917 Bending Boulevard. North end of the city. Now. Clevenger was very specific about the north end of the city. Bending Boulevard, like several other roadways, run north and south for miles. They cross the river that divides our city in half and continue on their way in both directions.

The city planners used a central point at the river as zero block and extended addresses in both directions. What that means is there are a shit ton of street numbers that have a counterpart on the other side of the river. There's a 3917 Bending Boulevard south of the river as well. My guess is that the gang doing the hit meant to shoot up *that* house and just drove in the wrong direction and killed the wrong people. Fucking idiots, but people are stupider than anyone besides me will give them credit for.

Clevenger can't come near this thing. I'm the closest thing he can get to doing it himself. He also must know Collins' style enough to think he won't get in my way. It's a great sucker punch. The PD sees Clevenger wanting their best assets to do the by-the-book investigation. He looks clean. Collins will turn over mountains of paperwork and thousands of dollars in man-hours for surveillance and canvasing.

Meanwhile, I'll have all the fun and faster results.

"You think Collins will figure it out?"

"Probably not. His worst trait is when he gets focused like this, he sees what he wants to see. I've been watching him. He's looking at all the elderly neighbors as if they have prison tats and a nine millimeter stuffed in their robes. He'll occupy himself with this street until it goes cold."

"Then I guess I'll leave."

"Keep out of the spotlight," Clevenger says as we shake hands. "We're on thin ice here."

"I know. And, once these retards figure out how fucking stupid they are, they'll roll a car out for the real address."

"We don't have much time, then," Graham says, his eyes like great white sharks.

"Be with your grandfather," I say. Turn to my car.

6

Just past midnight, Monday

South of the river.

I drive with one hand on the wheel. My .44 Magnum is in the other. Got to be ready in these parts. From the 3200 block down to the 5100 block of Bending Boulevard is exceptionally ghetto. There's some burnt-out industrial park-type stuff that bleeds in and out as well, some strip malls that have more bars than glass in their windows, lots of pawnshops, title loan joints and skanky fast food drive-thrus.

Whores with their poor fat distribution stuffed into leopard print wander about under the street lamps, peddling STDs. Here and there, clusters of young men eyeball any car driving down the road as if any one of them will roll down a back window and open fire.

It always seems work takes me south of the river. As a cop, this is where the good crime was. As a private detective, this is where the scum flees to because no one wants to chase it down here. Most folks have serious apprehension about following vermin this deep into the nest.

Bending Boulevard transforms from a five-lane sprawling drag to a two-lane cozy street winding through old, *old* neighborhoods. Lanes peel off one by one as homes become more prevalent. 3917 South Bending Boulevard is tucked back around a corner. I cruise by, pretending not to be taking in every detail as I pass. I get directly parallel to the home and look without reservation at it, develop the mental picture.

The plan comes with the look. There are three males sitting on the porch, feet up, smoking. Beer bottles on the railing. If I were to get out right now I'd smell weed. I've been at this too long to not be right about that. The house faces north. The west side there is a small strip of grass between houses that runs clear though to the next street over.

No lights on inside the home. The houses next door to each side seem quiet as well. Only one car in the driveway. No garage. No good lighting either. Wonderful.

I drive down the block. Turn left. Turn left again. Head-lamps off. Park. Leave it unlocked in case I need to clear scene in a hurry. Gun in hand. Crack my neck. Move.

Shadows are the only thing I want to be intimate with right now.

My eyes always one step ahead. Select the next bit of con-cealment. Someone nearby is grilling. No doubt munchies. Off in the distance a stereo is pumping hip-hop into the night. Crouch behind the topless husk of an old oak tree and see the new spot. Move. Into the strip of grass between the houses. Checking windows as I pass by. A lone, naked shrub is the only obstacle in the strip. I come up from behind 3917. The house next door has six gas meters attached to it. Rentals. 3917 only has one. Good. It's too small to subdivide anyways. Maybe seven hundred square feet inside. One story. The porch is on my left.

There were three males. The one in the center is the one I want. Crouched low, I stalk along the house until I'm beside the porch. The male now closest to me looked the biggest; probably three hundred pounds. The one on the far outside looked young. Little brother maybe.

These jackoffs consciously organize themselves in a tiered,

positions-of-power way. They idolize movies and establishments where powerful men appear as rulers. And by that I mean kings. Literal *rulers*. They surround themselves with their minions. That can take on a literal form when they move in groups. Or sit on a porch. I want the man surrounded by others. The central figure. The bet is he's the most powerful among them.

If my hunch is right—and this is me we're talking about, so it is—that also makes him the target.

Voices. The telltale long, high pitched inhale of someone dragging on a joint. Smell the ditch weed. Talking about some club. Some girl.

Blast off. Up over the rail. Fat boy sees me first. With his kicks up on the railing, he tries a full body spasm to get on his feet. Pistol whip across his mouth. Bridge of his nose. Three hundred pounds of lard and ill-fitting clothes make a deep *thud* on the wood of the porch. Across him. Elbow to the powerful male, who is all of twenty-five years old. It connects just above his temple and the stars he's blinded with follow him down to the porch. The younger brother ain't that young. Twenty-ish. He stands. Digs into his waistband. Pistol whip up side his head. Goes down to his knees. Sways; fights unconsciousness. A small gun slips out from his waistline and strikes the porch with a staccato note. A left cross snaps his head back and into the far railing. Blood everywhere. Collapses into a heap.

Younger brother's gun goes over the side into the yard. One eye keeps to the front door. The other eye to the powerful male. I roll him over. Toss his pockets. His own firearm, a shitty 9mm goes out into the yard somewhere. A pack of smokes, a lighter. Four cell phones. Must be a drug dealer. A utility bill folded in half. I look at the return address. Andre H. Moss. 3917 S. Bending Boulevard, Saint Ansgar.

Hello, Mr. Moss.

His wallet has his government assistance debit card. I take it. Drug dealers do this: they sell their junk and all the while claim unemployment. There's no sense in spending your poison-money on things like doctor's visits when the taxpayers can pick up that tab for you. Better save it for things like guns and a Lexus. Dealers take that as payment as well. A welfare card. A bus ticket. Pussy.

Moss also has a non-driver's license ID card confirming his name on the bill, ten dollars in cash—which I take because my smokes don't buy themselves—and two baggies with meth inside.

A note on clothing: some thugwear clothing companies sew concealed pockets into their shit. A pair of jeans will have deep, deep pockets running down the legs, or little hidey holes tucked behind a normal pocket. They do this the same way potwear companies will sew in small, easy to miss pockets for a dime bag or a dug out. Stashing pockets. Drugs, a pager, a small gun.

In one of these stashing pockets Andre has a nice, antique pearl necklace. Out of place on this guy. I take it as well. It might be nothing, but my finely tuned piggy sense says it's worth a second look.

Examine his hands, arms. Unkempt and long nails. Fake gold watch. A tattoo on the webbing between his pointer finger and thumb. Prison ink. He's got a teardrop under his left eye. Names tattooed in cursive on both sides of his neck.

Shirt up. Some usual gang graffiti that passes as ink on these fools. One scar on the outside of his torso that might be a small caliber entry wound. He stinks like bathing just isn't as sexy as it should be.

Amidst all this, my eyes move back and forth in a constant scan. Three hundred pound guy, front door, younger brother. Three hundred pound guy, front door, younger brother. Three hundred pound guy, front door, younger brother.

I give fleeting thought to taking Andre Moss with me somewhere else so we can talk. As I decide it's probably better that I do, he stirs. Consciousness floods back. Eye lids flutter. Licks his lips. He comes alive with a jolt of confusion and the remainder of adrenaline. I shove his arms under his body and drop both my knees onto his chest. Pinned. Muzzle to his eyeball. We do this here, then.

I grab his neck and shove his head backwards as far as it goes. Harder for him to scream that way.

"You shout, you die. All I want is to talk."

His non-gun eye rolls down and looks at me. He tries to speak but all it does is bare his teeth. Tries to be tough. I strike him on the forehead with the gun barrel; put it back in his eye.

"You got no one to show off for, Andre," I say, yanking his head side-to-side. "Your friends have checked out. Someone tried to kill you tonight but they got the wrong house. Who was it?"

"Man, I don't know what—"

Strike to the head.

"Try again."

"Cops," he says in the smart ass tone that any arrogant punk has. "Baby mamma. White people. Gang. They all want me," he says, trying to smile. A laundry list of potential enemies means he's doing something right. What a world he lives in.

"Gangs. Name them."

"Every gang in the world, bitch."

"Which one tonight?"

He wrenches his body and gets an arm out. I drop my piece onto his face. Grab his flailing wrist. He bucks his head; the gun falls off to the side. Cuts on his nose and inner eyebrow. Both my hands on his, I take his pinky finger.

"We're out of time, son," I say. A snap fills the cold air as his cutest finger finds a new angle to point in. My hand down to his head, shove it back under his jaw and push as far as it goes. No scream. I'll let the burn from the broken bone settle in.

"You answer my question and you get to dry swallow some of that meth in your wallet. It might numb the pain. Plus, the quicker you give me answers as opposed to this *gangbanger represent* bullshit the quicker you stop losing fingers."

He struggles against me. Like a snake caught by its tail he

whips as hard as he can. I look to his buddies but they do not stir. Once one of them does, this will get out of hand. Fast.

I pull his head up off the porch, slam it back down. His eyes jiggle with the impact. Next finger in hand.

"What'll it be, Andre?"

"Fuck you—"

Snap.

Hand to throat, pushing back. Struggle as a way to expel the pain from his body since I won't let him scream. I stop pressing so hard and I see tears cut a path down his face. Now we're getting somewhere.

Next finger.

"What gang?"

"I roll with the 39th Street Felons! My parole officer gonna know 'bout this! Motherfucker, you goin' in the pen and I got friends who gonna shower rape your ass—"

Head up off the porch, slam back down.

"Don't threaten me with butt-fucking, son." There's a certain decorum we follow, and cornholing isn't included.

39th Street Felons. Not what I was asking for but might be just as good. I still know some guys on the gang unit. They'll know who Andre's folks cross most often.

Andre groans, trying to fight back sobs. Rolls his head off to the side and spits. That's a great sign. He spit...and not in *my* direction. He might not respect me, but he knows the consequence of disrespect. We finally understand one another.

"Who tried to kill you tonight?"

"Don't know," he says with a hint of honesty. "Coupla gangs is out for me. We took some hood from the SA Crips. We cornered and jacked some fool who got crew in Los Carniceros or what the fuck ever."

"*The Butchers?*" I ask. The Los Carniceros are a Mexican gang who made their name decapitating the families of their adversaries. Gangs and cops went to war with them, and luckily for the world the Carniceros took some heavy losses. But they still exist.

"The street says Thuggie in Carnivore Messiahs is after me. That's bullshit."

"If they're after you, a drive-by is quite tame."

"Thuggie just got outta the joint. He's gettin back in the game but he's gotta lay low so he don't go back."

"Who is Thuggie and why does he want you?"

"He started the Carnivores. LaTrell something. He says I strong-armed his auntie or his nana."

"You robbed his grandmother?"

"Yeah. Bitch be cruisin' through my hood, she pays the toll. Fuck that bitch. I ain't in this business to help other peoples' grannies. Shit is simple."

"You robbed an old woman?"

"I said yes. Bitch ain't walkin through my hood and not know who owns it."

"What kind of guy robs an old woman?"

"I always let 'em know I mean business. That's how I run my show."

Let 'em know I mean business. Translation: *I use a gun.*

I look up, out into the street. Party is over.

"You know what Thuggie drives?"

"Eighty-one Buick Regal, up on hydraulics."

"What about an old Pontiac Grand Am? Dark body with a red driver's side door?"

"He got crew with that car, yeah."

"Didn't take them long to figure out they hit the wrong house," I say to myself.

"What?"

The car douses the headlamps. Crawling by. Back window down.

"Andre, you said something about paying a toll, right?"

"Yeah! That bitch—"

I throw an elbow across his eye socket and shove him full-body into the air. Into view.

He tries to scream as the night erupts into a cacophony of shrill barks. Street sweeper. Andre gets perforated. I duck and roll before they get me.

Bullets spray the house. I get behind the three hundred pound guy. Shove him up, use him as a wall and feel one bullet punch into him. Glass shatters. Wood *plinks* and gives way to lead. Snaps come alive all around and I make myself as small as I can.

Andre collapses in a pile, blood everywhere. The bullets stop the same time the car peels out and I move. Grab my heater and I've got one more thing to accomplish.

Andre committed the original sin here. He lived in the mirror address of Clevenger's grandparents. He committed the crime that put a bounty on his head. He got Eudora killed. He's now done. Toll paid. That end is clean.

The guys in the car are no doubt the same ones who rolled up on Clevenger's family.

Engine snarls. Tires squeal. I brace against the stair railing. Sights to my eye. One good shot. The shooter is in the backseat, driver's side. A single .44 Magnum roars into the night. Back windshield shatters. The shooter's head drops down. The driver freaks the fuck out and sideswipes a tree as he mashes the gas. Nearly loses control of the car. Swerves, over-corrects and swerves again. Takes the corner on two wheels.

Fatty took a round in his chest. His eyes are too glazed to be alive. Younger brother has at least one entry wound in his thigh. He hasn't moved since I punched him. Hard.

No looking back. I bolt back down between houses. Lungs burn. I swear behind every shadow there is someone waiting to shoot me. Nerves. Gun in hand, keys in the other. Get to the car, unlocked in case I need to clear scene in a hurry. Gun on the seat, ram the keys home. No headlamps for a quarter mile. I get it three times the speed limit within ten seconds. Dart through neighborhoods, head north.

PD will flood the new shooting. Once Collins hears the address he'll follow. I cross the Mannasmith Memorial Bridge back into the northland and start to think about Clarence Petticoat, his at-large rapist, Clevenger, calling Howard Michigan at five a.m.

The usual fare.

Ann Long Memorial.

The waiting room is small; quaint. Clevenger sits next to his ninety-two-year-old grandfather in a room where the walls are a psychologically calming hue of white, the gentle pattern of the carpet, carefully designed to avoid the appearance of being busy. Busy designs can irritate a person. Irate people take death notifications worse than calm people. Clevenger's grandfather looks calm. Defeated, but calm. His face, a formerly empty palette now scribbled by the hard pressings of being stunned. Stupefied. Numb and overwhelmed.

What a night. One minute you're sleeping next to the woman who you've been married to for so long you have to work to unearth a memory without her in it, and the next moment your house is alive with gunfire and screaming and bleeding out. Alive with death, that dirty whore pulling her veil of eternal sleep over your spouse.

Clevenger's grandfather is named Willibald, which impresses me just because he sounds like a legendary medieval swordsman. But now as I walk into the gulf of sorrow that fills the small room, he's a man who was proud five hours ago and broken now.

Clevenger looks up, his eyes a hard question. The thirst for revenge that floats to the top of a person's eyes, like the hunger of lust I have seen in other men's eyes, it occupies his face.

I nod. Half-smile.

Graham Clevenger exhales, long. He's been holding that particular breath since he got the word. Exhaling, the first time he has since the bullets ripped apart his family. He's got his arm around his wife Molly. He shrugs and pulls her tighter. She sees me, smiles. Lovely. I don't know if she fakes it or not, but when she smiles at me I feel welcome. If Graham were my son, Molly would make me proud as a daughter-in-law.

"Come. Sit with us." Molly is on the end of the waiting room couch. She reaches across Graham and pats the open seat. She grips her tissue a little tighter in one small hand, streaks of sorrow-black mascara cutting tiger stripes across it.

I near the open seat, see Willibald. The old man looks up to me, his eyes void of tears but only because he hails from a generation who still does those things in private.

"Hello, Richard," his voice, nails and ash.

"Hello," I say, look at Graham. He nods ever so slightly. I turn back to Willibald. "If it eases something inside, I heard from some cop-buddies that the men who did this got the address wrong. They went south of the river to get it right and were killed during the drive-by."

I rub my face. "The shooter is in a body bag. Maybe two."

"Did he have a wife?" Willibald asks, looking down at his gruff hands. "Do shitheads like that still respect marriage?"

"No."

He looks up to me, his face as honest as a child's. "You were married once, am I right?"

"Yes. Widowed."

He looks away and that word, *widowed*, it floats through the air like a spider's web and settles down upon him. It has him now; that definition fits his life. Widower.

"We have that in common, I guess. How does it work?"

I've spent my life pondering that. "It made me believe in God."

"You didn't before then?"

"If you met my parents you wouldn't either."

"Why then? After He took away your other half, why *then* did you believe in Him?"

Molly reaches across Graham and pats my hand, as if, since

she is the only living wife in our circle, she has to somehow fill a spiritual gap. "Two reasons. The first is because I need her. She is gone in this life, but in the next I keep hearing promises from the Holy Bible she'll be around. So I want there to be a heaven so I may have her again."

"I see," he says, looking off into some great distance that is beyond the waiting room wall. I can see he hopes that as well. To be reunited. A secret desire. Without facing me he says, "And the second reason you believe in God?"

"So I can get my hands on Him for doing that in the first place."

"You say that with conviction."

"I mean it with conviction."

After some time of being quiet, visiting with the doctor, people in and out, Graham taking some cell phone calls about the second crime scene, my best friend steps out of the room.

Molly rustles through her purse. "I need a coffee. Anybody else want one?"

I give her some cash. "This round is on me."

"Thank you, Richard."

She smiles again, and that's enough thanks for me. "If they have booze, make sure it finds its way into mine."

"Sure." Halfway out the door Willibald speaks up. "Molly." She stops, turns around. He stares at her for a second, says, "I want the same thing."

"Oh. Of course. Two spiked coffees from the hospital. Coming up."

"Good girl," Willibald says. Molly leaves and it is just us widowers left.

Willibald turns to me with the pace of a clock hand, ticking off the seconds of the universe with the authority of time itself. He says, "Getting your hands on someone, now there is something else we have in common."

"Do we?"

"Yes."

I nod and grunt. He smirks, and to my surprise he reaches into his jacket and pulls out a flask. "Something tells me this place ain't gonna mix our coffee right." He uncaps the flask, drinks. Hands it to me. I take a pull. Scotch. Good scotch.

"I smell gun powder on you," he says. "Thank you."

"Well..."

"Oh, bah," he says, waves a dismissive hand. "Just say *you're welcome*. A man my age can't do the things he should anymore, even to my detriment. Those shitheads would have gotten clean away with it if it fell on me to avenge to my wife."

"You're welcome." Quiet. I'm not used to thanks.

"That's a hell of thing, you know. As old as I am, unable to even the score for the woman I love. I pray you never feel this weak. This helpless. Like a baby. It tears a man apart."

"Cancer stole my wife," I say, not wanting to think about it. "Ate her from the inside out. I do know what you mean by being helpless. In my early twenties I was that helpless. I fought in a war. I killed men. But I couldn't kill cancer. I never will."

"I see," he answers, and it is good enough for me.

No conversation for a time. Then, out of the blue, he says, "Now, there's a concept for you, all right. *Getting your hands on someone.*"

I turn to him. "It's a hell of a thing."

He never meets my eye, just looks at that wall; at that distant place he has been seeing so much of tonight. "I arrived in Europe forty-three days after Normandy fell to the Allies. I was eighteen, fresh out of basic. Eudora and I got married on furlough and I headed straight into the dragon's mouth. She got herself a job at a war bakery; said she'd kiss every pie box that came off the line and went my way.

"Those fucking Krauts on the Eastern Front, freezing to death while they fought the Russians, they raped everything they came across. I heard their head Nazi doctor out there felt that raping young women was an acceptable morale deterrent against jacking off. Kept the homosexual desires at bay, as well. Can you believe it?

"I was eighteen, born and raised in Wyoming. Never really crossed my mind...the things evil men do. You get in war and all of a sudden whatever nightmares you had in the darkest parts of sleep become commonplace reality. You smell them. They soak into your clothes; keep you damp with their filth. They get their stink on you like mud in your boot treads. Rape as a moral deterrent. Only the fucking Nazis."

Another man's story about rape. Great.

"The Western Front seemed to be spared of the brunt of it, especially by comparison. But it happened. I know the French women got it. I saw a poor gal who had been beaten before they did that to her...and I grew up. Right then. Right there. Boot camp be damned. Going to war be damned as well. I matured into a harder man than the war could have otherwise made me. She wasn't particularly attractive. Not even that thin. But she had the parts for sex, so someone forced it. I remember how she just grasped her groin and moaned like she had been set on fire for a minute and put out. Left to suffer until Death swooped in with its talons. Just never came. Not that way, anyhow. She just agonized. And I remember how, even through her black and swollen eyes, her tears fell. It was raining out, and I knew the difference between the raindrops and her sorrow.

"Someone needed to pay."

He rubs his face the way I do: a long and drawn-out motion. A weary hand pressing hard.

"I waited. Found her in the infirmary a few days later. Did Graham ever tell you I could draw?"

"He said you made a living doing book covers, movie posters, custom work and the like."

"Yes." Willibald gritted his teeth. "She described the man to me. I drew him."

He met my eyes. There, in those old windows to his old soul,

I saw that thirst for revenge floating at the top. "And I found him.

"Several other squads had been drafted to take a few remaining rats' nests just to the north of where we were. A few weeks had gone by and I snuck off every chance I got to show the picture around. Something inside burned. I don't know what. Maybe nothing more than righteousness, if I may be so bold as to claim it.

"Every prisoner we took in. I held the drawing up to him, trying to force the pieces to fit. The curve of his eyebrows, the way his earlobes went straight into his head rather than dangled. Free as opposed to attached, a doctor once told me. Anyways, his were attached. Sharp point to his nose but his nostrils flared. She said he snorted. That sound was a trigger for her, I guess. She'd hear it in her memory and curl up. Some Kraut snorting. Lord save us.

"But those squads that cleared the rats' nests, they came back with a good bunch of yellow bellies who just dropped their rifles where they were and stood, arms reaching for the damn sky. What a bunch of pussies.

"Word came back real fast that our boys were marching a line of Krauts into camp. Said the line was as long as the Mississippi but smelled twice as foul and only spoke Pig Latin. So I waited. Bargained with another private to take my duty and I'd take his in the midnight shift so I could be there. Drawing in hand. Of course, I had Bessie, my BAR in the other."

Browning Automatic Rifle. Good man.

Willibald leaned back in his seat, smiled just enough to betray how smug he was in his moment, and said, "Our boys marched one hundred and nineteen Krauts back into camp. The man I wanted was number one hundred and ten."

"No doubt you had him arrested for war crimes."

"I donkey kicked him outta the line while hollerin' *rapist*. Bastard hit the mud and tried to scurry away from me. Crawlin' on all fours. The way he did a lot of things, I suppose. The other Krauts just froze stiff, probably worried that we were gonna treat them the same way we had heard they had treated the Jews or whatever.

"Anyway, some officer came chargin' up, wantin' to know what I was doing. I showed him the drawing, told him about the woman and all, pointed to that guy. Kraut started to cry. A bunch of Johnnys had come over, some to corral the Kruats and some to see what it was and if'n they could get in on it. The brass looked back and forth, back and forth.

"Looked at the Kraut and said *lemme see your chin*. You see, the French gal told me he had one of them clefs in his chin, deep as a canyon. The Kraut didn't want to show off his chin at all, and a lot of people thought that was guilt, pure and simple. But I had heard the snorting. He'd been snorting since he come walkin' by, the pervert. And I said so.

"I think I was the first to fire, but by the end there was so damn many of us who did it's impossible to tell. Anyone who didn't know what was happenin' took cover. Thought Hitler himself was leading a charge against us. Lord save us I got in a world of hurt over that killin'. But I never apologized. And I got the right man. No time in the brig either, I might add. Right is right. For me, that proves it.

"Richard, this world is fucked up, and the greatest and worst thing God ever did was give us free will. That Kraut used his to destroy a woman's life, and I used mine to make it so he couldn't do it again. Does that make me evil?"

"No."

"I never felt that way. 'Course, the wife, she used her free will to ignore the question the one time I asked her 'bout it. I decided not to think too hard on what her answer mighta been."

"Probably just moved that her husband wanted to defend the honor of a woman he'd never met. You went the extra mile for that French gal."

He laughed. One good hack. "Yeah. Sure." He drifted off for a while, said, "Yeah, sure," once or twice more.

Finally, while looking elsewhere, he said quietly, "Sometimes I worry I set somethin' in motion that day. While that Kraut earned the execution, I do admit what I did was out of line for what we as civilized people would call 'justice.' I worry whatever I set into motion that day...it waited patiently just like I did as that tour of prisoners came into camp. It waited patiently, and fucked me royally tonight."

"Nah," I said, weak as it was. Truth be told I started ticking off the laundry list of things I had done which came around to give my wife cancer.

He didn't say anything in return, and we just sat there for quite some time and pondered how we may have killed our wives.

7

Just before five a.m., Monday

A few hours' sleep is all that will come.

It's all I have time for anyways. I get up and turn on the stove burner. Make coffee the old fashioned way. Bottle of whiskey, spike the joe. Morning's first cigarette. I splash some water in my face and set my weapon down on the table. Take it apart. One hand begins to wipe down the cylinder and barrel, the other dials Howard Michigan's home telephone line.

His cell phone and business numbers have voice mail. His home line has no such thing. It rings. He forgot to disconnect, just like I told him. On ring seven he picks up.

"Richard, you filthy cocksucker—" his voice crawls along the line like it's the first thing he's said in an eon. Husky and thick with sleep, I can just see him on the other end slowly rubbing his forehead where a migraine is sprouting.

"Hey, I had a dream about you." My first words of the day as well, deep and tired.

"I'm hanging up now."

"Wait, wait, wait. Don't you want to hear my about my dream? It was nothing gay. Remember when I was a rookie and you'd have me hang out in the patrol car while you'd run inside and fuck somebody's wife? Well, in my dream I was in the car but it was a Zamboni for some reason and you were selling vacuums and then out of nowhere monkeys—"

"Goodbye, Richard."

"Hang on. Seriously. Are you sober now?"

"Yes. And if I'm not asleep again really fast, and I mean really *fucking* fast, I just know a migraine will be kicking up and this time it'll be all—"

"Tell me about this Clarence Petticoat."

"Damn you, Buckner." Deep breath. "Are you just gonna come over here and knock on my door if I cut you off?"

"What do you think?"

"Fine. One minute."

"One minute," I say.

A moment to recollect as he sighs with annoyance. I heard that a lot when we used to roll together. "I guess I never knew he was widowed. He always struck me as the playboy type. He hired me a few times to dig around on some broads he was dating. Usual kind of trim who hangs on rich men that they wouldn't touch if they weren't rich. Fake blonde, fake tits, decent legs, got their teeth fixed, low self-esteem and trying to make up for it now that surgery has made them pretty. He always paid on time. Was easy to work with. Didn't like no for an answer. You know he's a real estate guy. He's got an office up in the Burkhardt complex off of I-50. I haven't done anything for him in a while. There. Happy?"

"Mostly. Send me a list of the women you checked out."

"Fine. Later."

"Later is good for me. Thanks, Howard. Sleep tight."

"Choke on a dick, Richard." Click. Silence.

That's the Howard Michigan I know. I finish cleaning the gun and shower. I take a handful of aspirin. I don't really need it right now, but it's going to be a long day. Might as well get the jump on whatever pain is coming.

Clevenger calls as I'm driving to breakfast.

"Hello, Graham."

"Got some news about last night," he says, sounding a world more tired than I feel.

"Do tell."

"A friend in Ballistics stayed up through the night to examine the projectiles from last night. Same gun killed both Moss and Grandma." He pauses. Shifts his tone. "Richard, the words *kill* and *Grandma*..."

"I know, buddy. I hate how ugly this is."

Graham coughs the way men do when they're trying to avoid sounding weak. "The two guys on the porch with Moss, I don't remember names. One was shot in the chest. The bullet nicked an artery and a lung. Good shot. Dead. The other was ruled dead before he was shot in the thigh—flesh wound only. Seems he was struck in the head by something firm, possibly metal and punched in the face so hard it knocked his head into the railing. Cranial bleed.

"The gunner in the car was ID'd as Philip 'Shortie' Freeman. He's a punk out of the northwestern end with gang affiliations and two violent felonies under his belt already. He's nineteen. Covered in Carnivore Messiah tattoos. My detective said he took photos at the morgue and brought them to the Gang Enforcement bureau. The boys over there knew Shortie by name. Read his ink. Fuck that kid."

"Was he your original trigger man?"

"Both the driver and the passenger are pinning everything on him. Convenient for the survivors, but I think forensics will prove it. Shortie was hit once in the back of the head by an unknown caliber as they were driving off. The bullet passed through, grazed the passenger seat headrest and exited through the front windshield. Haven't recovered it. I'm guessing it was a .44 Magnum by how most of his head is gone."

"I can neither confirm nor deny, my friend," I say, pulling into a spot at a greasy spoon.

"Well, Shortie's friends treated him with gangbanger reverence. They took him to the ER at Regional. The driver honked a few times and took off. ER security got the plate off of security video, called PD immediately. A patrolman spotted the car heading northbound. Our guys did a felony stop."

I step inside the seat-yourself establishment and select a booth where I can watch the front door, the short order kitchen and my car. Habit.

"We recovered two Mac 10's, both with fifty round drum barrels. No wonder he was able to spray the houses," Clevenger says. "There was also a pile of shell casings in the floorboard. Probably from both shoots."

"Street sweepers," I say, scanning the menu. "I assume Collins is working this as well?"

"Yes."

"Has he questioned them yet?"

"They only said three things: Shortie did everything, we did nothing and we want lawyers."

"So be it."

Graham exhales long. "Richard, one thing though."

I'm weighing the difference between a bacon omelet and corned beef hash, say, "Sure, buddy. One thing."

"The gang bureau has already heard talk of retaliation. Hopefully the Messiahs blame Moss's gang and they make our work easy. But just because I'm paranoid, I want you to keep that fat head of yours low until this blows over. Got me?"

"If they somehow figure I'm the shooter out of all the enemies they've ever made, let it come. But for you, alright, buddy. I'll call this evening. I'm going to need some stuff from you."

"Okay. Thanks again, Richard."

"Hey. Every now and then one friend needs another to put some serious hurtin' on two rival gangs. Don't mention it."

We hang up. My waitress comes and I order.

Next on the list: Carla Gabler, the rapist's girlfriend.

8

0823 hours, Monday

I pinch another butt from my cigarette out the window and watch the house.

I parked across the street a few doors up. The neighborhood was blue collar back in the '70s. Now, it's ring-around-the-collar. Nothing fancy; matchboxes and one-story ranches up and down. Enough front yard to have a bad lawn, enough backyard to put a baby pool and chain up a pitbull.

Driveways big enough for two cars nose to ass, cracked sidewalks and concrete. Dreams to match.

Carla Gabler is standing at the edge of the yard as a sixteen-year-old girl hands her a toddler from the back seat of a still-running car. Carla receives the child and smiles, showers the little girl in kisses. The sixteen-year-old hands over a ratty diaper bag and leans over to give a very fake kiss to Carla. Both their cheeks touch and I can see Carla mime a smooch into thin air before the sixteen-year-old hops back in the car. She lights a smoke before she guns it off the curb. No looking back.

I see Carla stand there for a moment, radiant with affection for the innocent package in her arms. The little girl gives the love right back. The sight of the two of them together against the backdrop of this shitty neighborhood, the four square feet of brown lawn Carla has with her rental shoebox, the over-grown dead tree in the neighbor's yard, the twenty-pound piles of dog shit in the other neighbor's yard, the ramshackle chain link fence that seems to endlessly divide one house after another, all the accouterments that scream *white trash,* those two together are love.

The little girl has a plastic grocery sack in her hand. I see blonde and brunette doll hair hanging out. The girl slings her arm through the handle loophole in the bag and pulls it up to her shoulder as if it were a purse. In Carla's arms her feet dangle and she kicks them playfully.

Carla's face shifts some and she turns the little girl over in her arms to examine her diaper. Carla finds something there and becomes upset. It's not the look of a person who realizes they have to change a diaper, but rather the look of someone who realizes the diaper should have been changed an hour ago.

They go inside. I put my gear shifter to D and head out.

An hour later I knock on Carla's front door.

It cracks open, limited by the security chain. I see a green eye poke around the wood. Immediately smell years of cigarette smoke.

"Not interested," she says, her voice husky from all those cigarette smoke years.

"Ma'am, I'm not trying to sell anything—"

"Piss off." The door shuts. I stand there for a moment. I hate it when this happens. I knock again.

The door swings back open and the green eye returns. "Just so you know, mister, this neighborhood doesn't buy vacuums, magazine subscriptions or cookies and has no need for lawn care guys or a new roof. And some of these doors will just open and start shooting so you should just squeeze your linebacker ass back into whatever jalopy you came in and drive back north of the river where people got the money to have *Vogue* and mint cookies delivered. Got it? I'm doin' you a favor here."

I stick my card out. She doesn't accept it. "Ma'am, I'm a

private detective. You're Carla Gabler, am I correct?"

Silence. The eye hovers, doesn't blink. Then: "Get out. Whatever you want, you get out."

"Ma'am, I'm trying to solve a rape. Occurred twenty years ago while you were still in Happenstance. I was just—"

"You tryin' to scare me?" Her voice cracks. I can imagine she's intimidated—which is not what I want. I'm sure she's alone in the house with the toddler. She's a felon so she can't legally own a firearm but who knows. That never stopped anyone. Here's a man on her porch four times her size who knows where she lives, her name, her history. I'm sure she's wondering what else.

"I'm callin' the cops," her voice cracks harder. She looks back inside the home. I'll put good money that she looked at the little girl. She turns back. I see a tears watering up in the green eyes.

"No, I'm not trying to scare you. I just wanted to ask you about an old boyfriend. The guy you got busted with."

"Mickey? I haven't seen him in—" She stops. "He got out before I did. He—one day he just—"

Things are adding up in ways she doesn't want them to. Like when a doctor tiptoes around the word "terminal" but the patient gathers the clues together, Carla hears *twenty years ago, boyfriend* and *rape.*

"You don't mean—" she says, having fully lost her ability to speak in complete sentences.

"That's what I'm trying to find out," I say. Hold up a shopping bag from the little kids store eight miles up the way. "I got your granddaughter some things. Thought maybe she could use them."

Carla's green eye scans above and below the security chain, looks at the bag, looks at me.

"Who did you say you are again?"

"Richard Dean Buckner. I'm in the directory if you have one." I hand her my card again. Her small hand offers two fingers through the doorway. I gently slip the card between them. Skittish. I need her to talk with me. Everything has to be gentle.

She pauses at the door for some time. Then: "I'm not ready to talk about this."

"I understand. There *is* a time issue here, but let it sink in. Call me or, if I may, I'll just stop by tomorrow. Same time."

I sit the toy store bag down on the porch, next to the box of diapers. "For your granddaughter."

I walk back to the car. Get in. Hoping to hear her call out for me before I shut the door. She does not. I shut it. So loud right now. Back out of the driveway. Leave.

Damn it.

I light a smoke and try and think of a new avenue I can go down while I wait for Carla to fall in line. What I really should have done this morning is gone right to PD headquarters and petitioned for some DNA from the rape kit. At least start that paper trail nightmare.

Two miles up the road my phone rings.

"Mr. Buckner?" Carla says, timid but forcing her manners to the front. "Thank you for the new diaper bag and whatnot...I have some sweet tea if you'd like some."

Inside the home the little girl sits in the middle of the floor, playing with the new Barbies I bought her.

I sip sweet tea and study her. Perfect little hands, her bare feet with toes that look like they were rushed to be put on right before she was born, her small elbows and knees that are perfect replicas of our own, how her face is all curves.

"She's a doll," I say. I lean back, recall the only Carl Sandburg I know, and I don't even know *why* know it. "A baby is God's opinion that the world should go on."

"Thank you," Carla smiles at the poet's quote. I'll take credit for it, but it would be my luck she's his number one fan.

Instead, she says, "Absinthe, can you say thank you to Mr. Buckner for the toys?"

The little girl regards me with a very shy sidelong glance. Under her breath I hear her tender voice say "thank you" and then she immediately focuses on something else besides the stranger in her grandma's house.

"You're welcome, sweetheart." I look at Carla. "Her name is Absinthe?"

"Yes." Rolls her eyes.

"As in the alcoholic spirit Absinthe?"

"Yes."

"Green? Flavored by green anise and sweet fennel?"

"Yes. Grande wormwood. The Green Fairy. I know. I don't understand what my daughter was thinking," Carla says. "Jamie—my daughter, she got pregnant at fifteen. I was so furious. She made it through her sophomore year and then had Absinthe, dropped out. Got a job at a restaurant as a hostess."

"And the father?"

"Twenty-six years old at the time. Punk kid. I had him locked up for statutory rape. He signed away his parental rights for Absinthe the day she was born. He'll be out in another two years. Little shit is in the same prison as Mickey was all those years ago."

I study Absinthe for a moment and wonder what I would have been like as a father; then I blow it off because with the shape my wife was in when we dated, when we married, there was never a chance. I heard a woman once say as an experiment we should all list the people we'd be willing to have sex with. Those lists would be miles long. But then, she said, make a list of those you'd be a parent with. Those lists had a single name. Maybe less. Somewhere along the line people somehow forgot that one leads to the other, and look at the difference in the selection process.

"Sometimes gifts come out of bad things," I say. "I've seen it on the streets all the time."

"I agree," Carla says. "That's why I have Absinthe as much as I can. Jamie is so willing to pass off being a mother that she actually took a second job. I didn't mind; it gets me more time with my grandchild. Plus, Jamie is not interested in being a parent. That's not fair to Absinthe. I am interested, and truth be told, I'm better at it. More experience if nothing else. So this is our arrangement."

"Good for you," I say and I mean it. In my time I've seen so many single moms with small children slung on their hips who had no interest in loving the kid. Their interest stopped at the sex, which I'm sure was a one-night stand. And the kids I saw, those are the lucky ones who were passed over by the Abortion Fairy. Cruise through any ghetto stuffed with any example of the human race and know that out of all the kids playing in the streets, they're the surviving fifty percent or less.

No one can wait to blow their load, nor can they be any less interested in their own children.

"Good for you," I say again. "Maybe we can switch gears a little bit and talk about Mickey."

"Well, I'd rather you keep telling me how wonderful my granddaughter is, but okay," Carla says, rubbing out a cigarette. "So, who got raped?"

"A woman named Shelia."

"I see. Is she okay?"

Not too many details. If I assume the worst here and Mickey is the rapist, let's assume he lives here with Carla. I don't think he does; but assuming the worst he'll be home after his shift is over at five. Carla here gets all the dirty details out of me, passes them on to Mickey who thought he was in the clear. Now it gets more complicated.

Or, assuming Carla knows nothing about it, she might clam up when she hears the man she loved is now accused of raping a woman who later killed herself over it.

Not too many details.

"I haven't spoken with her. I think she's a lot better now."

"Good," Carla says, lights a new cigarette. Drags deep, blows out long and cleansing as if the act of doing so releases her pent-up tensions about her long-lost love Mickey Cantu.

"Mickey and I met at a bar. Sweet, sweet guy. Never hit me. Never really even raised his voice. He treated me like I rode in on a pumpkin that had been turned into a carriage or something. We lived together for a year. I knew he was a burglar but he never hurt anybody. I can't say that enough. He took good care of me. I was Jamie's age when I moved out. I had terrible parents. By the time I met Mickey I was jaded. The thought of being with a felon didn't make me bat an eye. I've got stories about old boyfriends if you want to know about *real* felons."

She drags off her cigarette, a long, slender feminine thing. Her nails are meticulous. She's pretty for her hard life and her fashion looks like she borrowed it from Miami.

"Anyways. Mickey. Like I said we lived together for a year and then I asked him to take me along some night. We were probably drunk and I just got a wild hair. I was a receptionist for the local telephone company at the time and they just had laid off four of us. They called it *cut backs*. So I had time on my hands. He didn't want to take me but I have my ways. He had been scouting a display home in a new neighborhood for a week or so. The builders were showing it off day and night so he and I posed as an interested couple although we could never afford it. The builders had stocked it with furniture and some electronics. If nothing else Mickey thought the display items were better than what we were living with so he figured it'd be a good score.

"We gave it a week so they'd forget us and see a bunch of new faces. Then we hit it one night. What we didn't know was there was an electrical problem earlier in the day and the builders had an electrician inside the house working until it was fixed. I can't imagine the overtime money they were paying that guy...but he was there.

"He stayed upstairs while we rushed around downstairs

grabbing things. He called the cops. We were busted red-handed. Charged with aggravated burglary. I was so pissed I pleaded not guilty just to cost the city money. Mickey tried and tried and tried to talk me into pleading guilty so I could plea down my sentence but I have a stubborn streak. I lost and became inmate number one-one-nine-seven-one-one-three. Mickey pled guilty and worked things a bit, as much as he could. That's how he got out before me."

"When did he get out?" I ask.

"Spring of '92. The bitch of it is with good behavior I got out like four months later. But I never saw him again." Twinges of regret surface in her eyes. It's been too long and buried under too many new regrets to be tears. Those, I'm sure she finished crying a long, long time ago.

"Can you be more specific?"

Carla retreats into her memory and begins to recount mundane events stitched together as the timeline of her imprisonment. I see her eyes drift up and off as her lips move with very quiet words. She ticks off on her fingertips.

"Well, I remember President Bush vomiting on that Japanese guy. There was the whole Dahmer trial. There was a big corrections officer house cleaning at Happenstance right around then. Male guards and female inmates. It was problem. Mickey wrote a letter and said probably half those CO's wound up at his prison. The Bosnian War started right about the time I got a phone call from Mickey saying he was out. I remember that pretty well because I wanted him to watch the TV and tell me where the hell this Serb place was. I can show you Hollywood, Vegas and New York City on a map but Bosnia and Serb-whatever? Forget it."

The Bosnian War started in the beginning of April, 1992. Shelia Petticoat was raped in the last week of April. Which puts Mickey out of prison.

"Did he say anything about burglarizing a new house?"

Carla looks away. Very pointedly. A tell. She exhales smoke

forcefully. Again, that cleansing. She scrubs the ashtray with her cigarette, as if it were a fingerprint she was trying to rub off or a bloodstain she needed to work out of clothing.

Occupied with her cleaning, she says matter-of-factly: "He mentioned he was 'looking at some employment' which was Mickey's way of saying he thought he had eyeballed a new place to hit. That's all. I swear."

She stuffs that butt into the growing mound in the tray and lights a new one. She stares at Absinthe, who now has the two dolls tucked into the little play purse I brought to replace the plastic grocery sack. She looks at her grandma, smiles bright and beautiful and then twists from side to side to show off her new bag.

Carla smiles for a long while, beaming at her second chance for a good daughter. Still looking away, she lets her smile fade some before she says, "That was the last time I heard from him. Then he just...disappeared. When I got out I looked for him, went and saw his family and everything. Everybody said that by May first, 1992 he was a ghost. Vanished."

She looks to her hands. "I loved Mickey Cantu very much. Flaws and all. No one ever treated me better. Years later I had Jamie, but I never loved her father. I never loved another man. Wherever Mickey went, he took that from me. He kept it when he vanished."

I stand. Carla mimics me, then holds out her hand for my empty glass. I give it her and say, "One last thing. Who was your PO when you got out?"

"Started off as a guy named Dan Martins, but after he made a pass at me and I blew him off, I eventually got shuffled over to a woman named Jean Jamison. Or Johnson. Jean J-something."

Dan Martins. He was a parole officer with the city. Actually, Dan says he had been making house calls with her as well. Dan said one night during some pillow talk, she was recounting her life. Telling him about the boyfriend she used to date who got her in trouble. Then she said something about him robbing my *house.*

I don't know Dan Martins but I make the play anyways. "Martins was known for sleeping with his clients."

"That's what I heard on the street." Carla says, walking to the front door. "Amazing how many folks you meet in the system. It's like buying a car you've never seen before being on the lot and when you drive around, you see 'em everywhere."

"You're right."

"That's how it was with Dan. Over the years I run into people, they knew Dan by way of parole. Always the same story."

I nod. I don't like the complication.

Carla gives me a genuine smile. "Anyways, thanks again for all the stuff for Absinthe. Really. You didn't have to do it."

"You're quite welcome," I say.

"Also, the Sandburg quote melted me about my granddaughter."

I knew it. Number one fan. I go on, "Hey, not to pry, but why would Dan tell people you two had a relationship?"

"If he did, he's a liar. I only met with him twice and both times were in his office. Then I was transferred. My heart was still very much set on finding Mickey. Plus, Dan was a sleaze. Looking back at life I picked mostly bad men, but Dan was too low, even for me."

"Okay. Again, sorry to pry." I step on the front porch and thank her for being so cooperative. She smiles in a sad way.

"Carla, if I find out anything about Mickey, good or bad, I'll let you know." I start to walk to the car. As I approach it this time she calls out after me.

"Just the good, Mr. Buckner. What I have of him is untarnished. Just let me know the good."

I look back. "I will."

I get in the car and leave.

Carla might be lying about a relationship with Dan Martins. I don't think so. Dan Martins might be lying as well. Could be.

Clarence Petticoat might be lying about the two of them.
Probably. My gut says it.
Probably.

9

1100 hours, Monday

I call Captain Rose MacHowell at the PD. She and I were never an item but I think there was a time where she would have obliged me. This was back in the day when night sticks were still one solid piece of wood and your portable radio was a better offensive weapon than just about anything on your belt.

"Hello?"

"Rose. It's Richard. How are you?"

"I'm just great, Richard! Things are great. They have me over at Precinct 3 now. I come in and knock out all the paperwork that I can and then after roll call I spend a couple of hours out in a car. I missed it. Did you hear that my oldest is getting married?"

"Cassandra?"

"Yes. Her fiancé will be graduating state this year. He's got a job lined up. She has one more year left and will finish. His company has branches in Denver, Chicago, Atlanta—" Rose continues on. Sweet gal. I tune her out and wait for a momentary break in her rapid-fire blabs to get around to what I want. The reason I originally called Rose is because, up until her transfer to Precinct 3, she was the Records captain.

In the Saint Ansgar PD, the evidence locker falls under Records as well. If anyone can grease wheels for me into getting the DNA from Sheila Petticoat's rape kit, it's Rose. I fill her in on

63

what I need and she says she can probably make it happen as early as Wednesday, but Friday at the latest. I'll take it.

We say goodbye and I start making phone calls. Playing telephone, creating links in a chain from me to a guy who knows a guy who knows another guy who works in the same office as Hank Madison. I get his extension. Catch his voice mail. *Hello. You've reached the desk of Sergeant Madison with the Saint Ansgar Police Department, Precinct 5. I'm unavailable to take your call but please leave your name, number and a detailed message after the tone. If this is urgent, please press the star key. You will be transferred to the Precinct switchboard and they can transfer you to my cell. Thank you.*

Star key.

"Precinct 5 switchboard, how may I help you?" A pleasant female voice.

"I need to be transferred to Sgt. Madison's cell phone please."

"And your name, sir?"

"Richard Dean Buckner."

"Ohhh." Drawn out. Spit out. Like she bit into something sour. Seems the switchboard operator knows me. Bitch. "One second."

Cut to God-awful hold music. New Age Jazz.

Thirty unbearable seconds later and I hear ringing. Thank the Lord.

"Sergeant Madison."

"Hank. It's Richard Dean Buckner. Long time."

"Buckner. Holy shit. How are you?"

"As good as a burned cop can be. I was hoping I could sit down with you and talk."

"Sure. When?"

"How about now?"

"Now I'm in a drive-thru, waiting to order."

"Skip it. Lunch is on me. You name it."

"Wow. You must want to talk. Sure, why not?"

* * *

Madison named the shittiest gyro stand in all of Saint Ansgar.

It's a Greek taco truck. I've eaten at roach coaches before and never minded a bit of it. But this, much like Disney World, being on trial for brutality and asking a gal out on a date after I've arrested her for DUI, is an adventure I'll only do once because of the poor experience.

We get our food. Lean on the bumper of my car. I don't want the smell inside the vehicle, nor do I want something to slop of this pita and wind up in my lap or staining the interior. I have standards.

"So, I wanted to ask you about Clarence Petticoat."

Madison takes a bite of his gyro and raises an eyebrow. "Really? You looking to buy a house from him also?"

"Did you buy a house from him?"

"Almost ten years ago. Is he your agent? I thought he was mostly doing commercial stuff now."

"No. No house. He's my client. He said he knew you. He said you were an old friend."

Madison wipes his face and smiles like he was just fed a line of shit. "He was our realtor. And he was a cheese dick at that. As a guy, I mean. He was a shark in the real estate game. But, I first met him when we walked into his office. Almost ten years ago. I guess that qualifies as 'old,' but it was business. I think 'friend' is stretching it."

Hank smirks, looks me in the eye. "All that fucking guy did was ogle my wife. The only thing I liked about him was how he got us into our place. Other than that, he can fuck off."

"You're not friends?" I set my food down. "I want to be clear on this."

"No. We didn't hang out together, go for beers, play on the same softball team. We never had him over for dinner. You and I are closer friends than he and I were, and I haven't spoken to you in how many years? Why? What did he say?"

"So you didn't recommend me to him within the last week or two? To hunt down the man who raped his wife?"

"No, Richard." Very pointed. "I don't know anything about a rape. I didn't know he was married. Hell, whenever my wife was in the room, he'd be checking her out and whenever my wife would leave the room he'd brag about all the tail he was pulling. Why? What did Petticoat say?"

Another buddy of mine sent me to you. Hank Madison. He said you were the kind of guy who could walk into maximum security in the prison and those felons would step back. Hank said you've earned that reputation.

I light a smoke. "In early '92 his home was burglarized and during the course of events his wife was assaulted. She was raped. Eventually she killed herself over it. The case went cold. You remember Trevor Gillispie?"

"Yeah," Madison says. "Suicide. Divorced over his gayness. And why did they send a burglary dick to work a rape?"

"Right. Gillispie investigated. Went cold. That much is true. So now, all these years later Petticoat says he's getting major surgery next week and his odds are so-so at best. He wants that rapist dug up and in jail. He's shelling out big bucks for fast results. He said you're an old buddy who said if anybody can get it done, it's me. Which, of course, is true."

"He said that, huh?"

"Yes, he did. He said you told him I was the kind of guy who could walk into maximum security and those felons would step back. That's my reputation. Again, true."

"I haven't spoken to him since we bought the house. I sure as hell didn't talk to him about you in the last week or so."

"Interesting. Any idea why he'd lie about it?"

"He knew I was a cop. That's about it. I know you, but it's not like I talk about you to folks I meet in the course of my day. Although, everybody—including me—still tells the story about when you served the warrant on that child molester and the guy ran away. Right out the window."

"Davis something. That was fun," I say. It was.

Once, back in the day I did some extra credit work on a warrant task force. We served a child molester living in Saint Ansgar that some Three Mile High detectives had connected to a series of new sex crimes. Davis's apartment was on the fourth floor. I knocked on the door, he opened it a crack and I kicked it in. The freak took one look at me, said, "Oh my God, not *you*. Anybody but you. I know what you do to guys like me," and took off running. Well, it was actually a half-prance but it was the best he could do. He also screamed about four times, each one sounding like Michael Jackson getting fisted. I had three cops behind me who heard the whole thing.

I went after him. Davis took one look over his shoulder, saw me and changed course. I think he was running towards the fire escape until he saw how close I was. Instead, he ran right to a plate glass picture window that overlooked the street below. He went crashing right through it. No hesitation. One long King-of-Pop-getting-fisted scream followed him all the way down. The pavement beneath greeted him with firm, open arms. Case closed. Morbid, but hilarious. I'm glad that story still gets told.

I guess I do have that reputation.

"I don't know, Richard," Hank says, using thumb and forefinger to pull slices of lamb-flavored particle board from his gyro. "Petticoat is having surgery next week and he'll die? Why not just wait until after? If he survives, he's got his whole life to find out. If he dies, he can just ask God who did it."

"The more I learn about this guy, the more it seems like he's not going to get a lot of face-time with God before he's sent on his way," I say. That also gives me an idea about the surgery.

"For that matter, why not start this sooner?"

"Petticoat said he got a tip from a friend last month. Gave the case some momentum."

"So he skipped the police? Went right to you?"

"Yeah. Dedicated personal service, mostly."

"I guess I can see that," Madison says. "Although, the whole maximum security analogy makes sense to me."

"Oh yeah? Why's that?" I'm not hungry anymore, and not just because of the food either.

"He was a prison guard."

I look at Madison like there is some big joke he's in on and I am the butt of. "What?"

"Yeah. Petticoat used to be in corrections before he was in real estate. Quite a career jump."

"Where at?"

"We talked about it a little bit during the house thing. I remember he said a couple of places."

"Happenstance Women's Correctional?"

"Yes!" Madison snaps a finger. "Happenstance. How could I forget that name? Then there was another one. A male prison."

"Did he say why he switched?"

"No."

There was a big corrections officer house cleaning at Happenstance right around then. Male guards and female inmates. It was problem. Mickey wrote a letter and said probably half those CO's wound up at his prison.

I look off into the distance and two seagulls steal a piece of trash from a third bird. Then those two white-feathered rats peck each other until only one remains with its worthless prize.

"I bet I know why."

10

0600 hours, Tuesday

I walk into the lobby of the University hospital trying to look as caring and concerned as I ever could.

It isn't much.

I walk to the bathroom. I've done undercover work, but that was for dope. This requires a special Boy George skill I don't have. I loosen my necktie considerably, undo the top three buttons on my shirt, then untuck the whole thing. Spit shine the toes of my shoes real quick.

A guy walks in behind me, looks at the stalls. I turn around. "Hey, bro, you got any cologne?"

"What?" he asks. He looks like he's been up all night. His wristband has mother/baby visitor on it. Long labor, I guess.

"Cologne? I need a spritz...or whatever the word is."

"Nah." He gives me a weird look and goes to a stall. I shrug, leave.

Hank Madison gave me an idea about Petticoat's surgery. I walk to the gift shop. A female employee is just opening the doors for business as I arrive. I blow past her, snatch a GET WELL balloon and a stuffed teddy bear without so much as halt my stride going in. I go to the register and wait for the woman, who is still flipping around the CLOSED/OPEN sign.

She waddles across the small gift shop floor, squeezes her considerable mass behind the counter. She's already out of breath from shifting about her gigantic weight. I pay and leave. I walk right from there to the Admissions door. Into the waiting room. Another woman is behind a secretary's desk. I go up to it, bear and balloon first.

"Hello. May I help you?" she asks. Young. Like twenty. Homely but thin. Glasses, straight brown hair.

I've had worse. Much, much worse.

"Hi," I say, squeezing the teddy bear for effect. "My name is Joe Proctor. My romantic partner is Clarence Petticoat. Clarence T. Petticoat. He's supposed to be having heart surgery today. His mother is bringing him up here—*she doesn't know about us*—I was hoping to see him. He asked me to wait until later but I can't. I just can't. I—" I have to swallow hard, "—love him too much."

The secretary begins typing away as I ramble off my sob story. As I figured, what she finds makes her eyebrows scrunch together. She types some more, scans the data. Types a third time.

"Mr...?"

"Proctor," I say. Lean in.

"Mr. Proctor, you said Clarence Petticoat. Right?"

"Yes."

"I don't see a Clarence Petticoat in our system. I don't know what to say." She starts to look around for help.

Before she goes and gets a manager who might be more concerned about HIPPA law than my bullshit gay relationship, I say, "Well, miss, I used to do this also. Data entry, records keeping, phones, that kind of thing. Maybe I could make some teeny-weenie suggestions?"

She just looks at me and says, "Sure."

"He said the University hospital. I could have the date wrong...but I doubt it. Maybe you could check the entire week's schedule?"

"Sure. We should have all the scheduled procedures in the system...let's see..." Keystrokes, more keystrokes. She sits back, types something else. Huffs out.

"I'm not seeing Mr. Petticoat slated for anything cardiovascular or otherwise in the entire month. I'm so sorry, sir. I'd hate to ask you to call him but I'm just not sure what I can do."

He lied about Dan Martins and Carla Gabler. He lied about a potentially lethal surgery. What else now? What the shit is going on?

The young secretary looks up and sees my face. She doesn't say anything. I can't queer-up this kind of fury. The girl believes my boyfriend is lying to me about something. Worse. A client is lying to me about something. Something tense that might end poorly.

"Never mind." Ice. Finished. I push away from the counter.

"You're welcome," she calls after me.

I walk into the lobby. A large cardboard box is set up to collect clothes and toys for children in the hospital burn unit. I drop the teddy bear inside. I walk out the front door and let go of the balloon. It sails off into the gray morning sky off towards a cold death somewhere alone.

Something is happening next Monday that requires this whole thing to be wrapped up. Something Petticoat felt he had to lie about. What was he planning on doing if I found out he lied?

I should ask him.

At gunpoint.

11

Running around. Mundane.

I meet with Rose MacHowell at her new office in Precinct 3. She has all the paperwork required for me to request a DNA sampling from Sheila Petticoat's case. All nice and neat. Everything I need to sign is highlighted. Marked with an *X*. It still takes twenty minutes to go through.

We catch up for a while and I ask her to get ahold of her husband so I can take them to lunch. We meet him at a nice place where the appetizers are forty dollars and sodas are not on the menu. Lunch is pleasant. Rose has her shield displayed on her belt and her compact semi-auto handgun on her hip for the world to see. My iron is stashed under my jacket and I wonder if the wait staff can see it. I'm always curious how sneaky I am with it.

Rose, her husband and I part ways at the restaurant's front door. She says she'll get the paperwork filed today and expedited as fast as she can.

"Hopefully no later than Friday," Rose says, patting me on the shoulder. "Friday by the very latest."

I pull up in front of Petticoat's office, ready to acquire some answers, even if he has to eek them out around my squeezing mitts.

The office complex is very modern. It can't be older than a few years. Three stories. A pediatric dentistry practice occupies all the first floor except for the building lobby. The second floor looks like it has lawyers. The third has accountant next to one person's name. Petticoat has a corner space. I take the stairs.

His office door is closed, locked. A printed sign is attached to the door reading CLOSED and then a phone number. I call the number. Office line. I hear the fucking phone inside ring. Aggravating. Who tells people the office is closed but still wants them to call the unoccupied office? I dial his cell phone. On the second ring he answers.

"Mr. Buckner. How are you?"

"Clarence. I stopped by your office. I want to talk to you."

"Oh, sorry. I'm at the hospital. They want to run a bunch of tests before the operation. Blood work, EKG, you know the type."

I hear a ghostly noise in the background. I know what it is, but I need to stall him so I can hear it again. To make sure.

"The University hospital, right?" I ask.

"Yeah. Good folks."

"You might want to reconsider who cuts you open," I say. "I hear that hospital doesn't have the survival rate the other area hospitals do. Just saying."

"I'll be fine. I actually have to go. They'll be keeping me overnight."

"Maybe I can come by and talk to you there."

"I think it's going to be a hard night, Mr. Buckner. I've been on a downhill slide for the past few days. Stress is really getting to me. They say I just need some rest. I'm hooked up to some machines—"

There is the noise again. A hollow, metal howl like a specter coming down a hall. I know where he is.

"You sound so full of life. I figure a man who is going to have such a risky operation should cough or something."

Petticoat gives me two little squeaker coughs. "Happy?"

"Okay," I say, heading back out to my car. "I just wanted you to know I've requested the DNA sample from the PD. With any luck I'll be able to take it to a private lab that can run it against any DNA on file. I can only hope in the past twenty years the rapist has been arrested for something—*anything*—because then they'll have taken a sample from him. If so, we'll get a hit."

"Great. Just great. I've gotta go—"

"And Carla Gabler was a dead-end. She says she hasn't seen her boyfriend since they were locked up."

"Mr. Buckner—*Richard*, I need to hang up now. The nurses—they're getting on me for using a phone inside the hospital. You know. It may interfere with some of the machines and I—I need to go."

There the noise is a third time. Motherfucker.

"Not a problem, big guy. You get some rest. Take care of that cough." I hang up.

Dig in my trunk. I have a toolbox. Open it. Inside there is the usual stuff that anybody would have: duct tape, a drill, a straightened coat hanger, door wedges, lock-picking tools, a couple of cheap cell phones I've converted to listening devices, latex gloves, a couple of empty syringes I could fill with things like Drain-O or turpentine, some key blanks for bump keys, a gun. Probably some screw drivers and a hammer. Regular stuff.

I smoke a cigarette and go back inside. Gloves on. Pick the lock. Enter.

Inside the office a quiescence whispers through. I, in turn, walk with silence sewn onto the bottoms of my feet. Just in case.

The haunting ghost sounds behind Petticoat were the sounds of the rail train. The echoing squeals of metal on metal as they rub their smoothed surfaces at sixty miles an hour. The lilting hum of the train passing through a tunnel. You don't get that in a hospital room.

He's heading to Three Mile High. The rail doesn't run through town; it connects our two cities and that's it. Lying about that as well.

Plot point: for whatever reason Petticoat wants me to think he's ill. It gives him a convenient excuse to put a deadline on me. So him lying about being on the train might not mean anything by itself. It goes with the cover story. Wherever he is, he'll want me to believe he's in the hospital.

Of course, it might be very significant he's heading to Three Mile High. I tuck that in my mind and scan the office.

The hallway door opens into the secretary's space and waiting room. Nothing more than a welcome mat and a desk. By the look of the desk Petticoat doesn't think much of his secretary. She must be ugly or he's already fucked her. I don't think he's the type to hire a dude secretary. Even a homo one.

Pictures and reference letters all over the walls. Thank you notes, some from recognizable names and companies to boost his credibility. Nothing says worth-the-money like an autographed picture of a pro athlete thanking you for whatever service you did. I see four in Petticoat's front room. A couple of photos side by side that show a brown field of flat, barren earth as a before picture and next to it an after picture with a building constructed there. Manicured lawns, landscaping, lighting. Real estate development.

There is a drafting room. Nothing more than a box space big enough for five folks to stand around a table, pointing to a blue print and feeling self-important. The walls here are covered in artists' renditions of various projects. Schematics. Aerial views.

Petticoat's office is locked. Deadbolt. I pick it as well. One desk, two visitors' chairs. Window behind the desk. Blinds closed. More bragging material on the wall. One file cabinet. I search it. Filled with real estate contracts, form packages ready to be filled out, an open bag of candy, a canister of coffee, some rubbers. Ahhh. What an animal Petticoat is.

I sit down behind the desk, fire up the computer. It comes

right on; no security password to boot up. Good. As far as security goes, I hope he has all his faith in the two locks that precede the room. Makes my job easier. I'm not very good at cracking passwords.

The desktop loads up and I start combing through everything. File after file, document after document and download after download. He has four video games installed on the thing, enough pirated music to open his own record store and of course, so much porn it would take an entire forensics team working in shifts to view them all, searching for underage participants.

In other words, his computer looks like any middle management's PC except Petticoat doesn't have a boss to answer to about any of it.

But nothing that screams *next Monday* or *rape case*.

I open up his Internet browser and look at his bookmarks. I look at his search history and there's a lot of stuff I'd relate to his job, plus the porn. There are several maps provided by search engines. I click on one. Satellite photo. Just another brownfield waiting to be developed. There are several like this. Some are full constructions, some not. I assume he's looking at the surrounding area, checking to see how good a location it is.

Some are here; some are in Three Mile High. All told, there's a shit ton. I highlight, cut and paste them in an email to myself, then go back to the search history and delete that one page. I'll comb through them later. Something tells me Petticoat is going to Three Mile High today to conduct business. I go back to the most recent Three Mile High listing he's been looking at. Brownfield. Huge, huge brownfield in the middle of nowhere.

Email. No password protection. Nothing except an icon on the desktop. I click it, it sends and receives. I sift through the folders and un-emptied trash can.

Now here's something. Clarence T. Petticoat is being blackmailed.

12

CP—the usual time and place next week. The price is up to thirty K to buy silence. I strongly encourage you to make the right decision. Failure to do so will result in the police discovering your immense culpability; meanwhile I walk away scot-free.

God bless.

Scrappy-Doo

Rapist. *Usual time and place. The price is up.* Petticoat's been paying him for a while, and some good chunks of change if it's gone up to thirty thousand. *Buying silence and immense culpability. I walk away scot-free.* If it is the rapist, he's already walked away scot-free. Why come back now and risk it all? Greed. Simple greed. Scum rob each other every day for enough pennies to make a cover charge and dollops of low-grade dope, let alone hefty sums like these. But what culpability does Petticoat have in his wife's rape? Surely he didn't arrange for the sexual assault to occur. Especially with him being present.

It could be that when it went down Petticoat didn't fight and instead just let it happen. I can see him being a pussy like that. Or maybe he didn't *want* to help. He might have, essentially, thrown her to the wolves. Or maybe he hired a hit man for his wife who didn't kill her. Instantly, anyways. However it shakes out, this sheds a lot of light.

The email is from a cheap domain email server that could be run by anyone, anywhere. I do a search for any others. None. Deleted. I right-click the email itself and select *options.* I find the IP address the email was sent from. There are websites that trace IP addresses as far back they go. True hackers and other savvy folks have ways to run the address around enough to effectively disguise it beyond the layman's capabilities. I'm not a PC genius but I have some tricks.

I run the IP address through a couple of tracing sites and they all show up with the same registered telephone number. Could be a Smartphone, but any blackmailer who has the playbook down before he steps foot in the game will use some anonymous third party hardware to do this. Using one's own phone—except a throwaway—will be traceable. Any blackmail sent from an email address that isn't something like *John@Brand X Mail* is suicide.

I plug the telephone number into a search engine. It comes back to a business. Net café. Corner Bistro. I call it, if for nothing else just to make sure it's not a front. Blackmailing for this much money doesn't put something that extensive out of the realm of possibility. One only has to register the number to a name and put it on a search engine. No one says it has to exist.

Female voice: "Corner Bistro, how may I help you?"

"Hey," I start, making something up on the fly. "You guys have hot sandwiches and wireless Internet, right?"

"Yes, we do."

"Great. Where you at?"

"Corner of Forty-sixth and Sweet Gum. Corner Bistro."

I hang up. Go back out to the car. Get a listening device and some computer software an associate gave me.

Back inside I rig the listening device to the computer. There, it has a power supply and that won't run out like a cell phone battery will and it conceals better. I install the software that will enable me to remotely have access to Petticoat's desktop. Now I can fish through his emails without breaking into his office every time.

I re-open the latest blackmail note and hit reply. I type:

> Scrappy-Doo:
> Let's do it early. Got stuff to do on the usual day. I'm not meeting at the usual place, though. For thirty K you can adjust to my schedule. Thursday morning, 9a.m., the comic book shop on 20th and Grand. I'll be at the city bus stop in front. Don't bother trying to change it. You're starting to not be worth it.
> CP

That should do it. Hopefully this guy will take the bait. And be slightly pissed. Blackmailers—like most criminals—desire cooperation and respect over most else. Bank robbers might not be opposed to killing someone during a heist, but it complicates things immensely. They'd rather folks just pile money into a bag and stay face down on the linoleum. Same thing here. The blackmailer will not take lightly to his arrangement being changed. Complications. Sudden alterations leave little room for planning on his part, and control goes out the window. For all he knows Petticoat is luring him into a trap.

And of course, it is.

I pack up and go. Corner Bistro. Eyes peeled.

13

Stakeout.

I'm parked across the street from the Corner Bistro in a shady spot. Here a gentle shadow rests across the vehicle and keeps the worst of the spring sun at bay. Windows down let just enough of a cool breeze inside. God is in the little things. I've sat in plenty worse spots on sweltering days for a week or more at a time, looking for something that never arrived. So this is quality.

I have Petticoat's email opened up on a tablet riding shotgun. If and when the bad guy replies, I'll have it.

I'm gambling on a few things here, just because they're all I have. The bad guy can check his email from anywhere, but he'll be more discerning when it comes to sending one. I'm gambling that he comes here to do it. If he doesn't, I'm shit out of luck. Why this place is anyone's guess. Our rapist might not drive and this is the closest place within walking distance. He might work here or is dating someone who does. He might just like their brew.

It'd be nice if the rapist would just walk in there, read my reply and throw a fit. Come stomping out. Make a scene. But in reality, out here on the street, it is just a comfortable wave of face after face coming and going. I try and memorize them all so when the new meet comes at the comic book shop—assuming he shows—I'll be able to ID him on approach and head him off.

Take him someplace where we can talk.

The hours pass this way. Shadows leaning heavier to one side than I'd like. I call a sandwich shop down the block. For a ten-dollar tip they exit their front door, walk six storefronts down and deliver to my car window.

And more hours pass this way. No reply email. My lower back starts. I can feel my stubble grow into a full beard.

I look at the clock as the bistro draws its shades and flips its sign from open to closed. I pull away, dreading the funeral tomorrow.

14

Wednesday morning

The world overhead seems to know when a funeral is coming.

It builds a fabric of gray, of disappointment and regret and stretches it from horizon to horizon. The breeze brings with it immaterial icicles; little shards just to nip and bite even now in warm weather. Rain cavorts in protesting masses, still swirling in the storm clouds above. Waiting for the bomb bay doors to open.

Molly hugs herself and leans into Graham. "I swear this is the coldest Wednesday morning ever."

A single streak of lightning snaps in the mounting turmoil. It forebears a message from its brethren: we are coming...and in greater numbers.

This rent-a-pastor better hurry.

Graveside. Clevenger and I stand ridged against the winds. The small strip of hair still clinging to Willibald's otherwise nude head stirs in the breeze. Those flirty, miniature gales, running their distracting fingers through his remaining comb-over hair while his wife is interred. Bitches can't even wait for Eudora to be in the ground before they play with her surviving husband.

Willibald looks up to uncooperative weather, snickers. "I made arrangements for this to be fast. Only took a couple of days, you know."

Graham and I look at one another. For a murder victim, Eudora did get buried quickly. But, I guess it was cut and dry.

"I also made my own arrangements," Willibald says, giving a lifeless pat to Graham's elbow. "Keep you from worrying about it."

"Grandpa—"

"Quiet now. It's your grandmother's time."

An eternity passes by as the thunderheads loom and threaten. The pastor, part of the package deal with the funeral home, drones on and on like he knew anything about Eudora that Willibald didn't tell him five minutes before the whole thing started. So fake, trying to sound so sincere. So deep and comforting. So plastic. He could sell rust buckets, crack-cocaine or condoms to toddlers with his line of spit-polished horseshit.

Then all at once the funeral party clicks the ratchet that barks with a startling noise, lowering the casket. Each *tick* on the teeth of those gears puts a gulf between Willibald and his wife. I know that void.

And people peel off. One by one. Small groups. Vanish, like ghosts who have fed to their fill on the sorrow here. Given their marching music by the descending ratchet.

Pull up their collars. A dull mass of black coats and umbrellas being toyed with by incoming winds.

Mumble. Look at the ground. Step over flowers that have fallen from a grave they adorned. Leave.

I kneel, gently take the flowers. Put them back upright on the woman's grave marker from where they fell.

"She has the same name as your wife, right?" Clevenger, behind me.

"Yes."

"Soft spot?"

"I don't like seeing people treat our dead like that."

"*Some* dead, you mean."

I smirk. "There is a difference between decent dead people and the dead people we see."

"Right." Clevenger smiles some, looks back at his grandfather. His face relaxes into sadness. Another streak of lightning overhead races along on its electric highway, *booming* like a Howitzer.

Willibald sits in a wheelchair, dressed nicer now than any other time in life. Still. Hands resting in his lap, comforting one another. Breathing in and out because that is all he knows how to do now. All but a few dedicated people have left him to his thoughts.

Molly's hair snaps in the wind; fingers from the wind playing like catty bitches trying to muss up the prettiest girl out there. She holds Willibald's arm and rests her head against his shoulder. All I can see is that man as a young soldier, being steadfast for that French woman he avenged. I wonder if her head laid on his shoulder the same.

I walk beside Clevenger, staring at that sight. "He's strong."

"He's lost."

"Yes."

"You think he'll be a widower long?"

"No."

"I feel like a small man, or even a bastard for saying this," Clevenger says. A deep breath. He rubs his eyes, looks away. "I don't want him to be."

"He's lived a long life," I say. "He's made his mark. His legacy. He's fought evil, he's saved lives. He's made a home and a family. He's passed on everything he's learned. What he found when he arrived, he either left intact or better when he left. Don't feel small. His circle is coming complete. When those two ends meet, be there to tell him to go. Anything else would be petty."

I put my hand on Clevenger's shoulder. Squeeze. "And you're not petty."

A long time passes as the storm clouds gather their troops overhead. "Thank you."

I look along the edge of the cemetery. Another funeral way

off. Headstones scattered about. Acres of folks with nothing better to do than leave their families behind in this life. An occasional tree reaches up to the sky, calling out for a precious drink of water.

I shuffle along, cars pulling out into the street. Across the way I see a young man standing there, hands in his pockets. Hat cocked off to the side; brim as flat as a carpenter's wet dream. He stares on in our direction for a moment, then a crowd of mourners passes between him and my line of sight and he's gone.

I shrug it off. Punks and thugs are everywhere I look right now when I'm with Willibald and Graham.

"See a ghost?" Graham asks.

I shrug. See Molly and Willibald stopped up ahead, talking with friends of the family. "Nah. I'm seeing things in the shadows."

"Yeah. You're seeing ghosts."

"I worry they're real."

A thunderclap rips across the sky. I see raindrops. Slow in a wide pattern. But they have intent. I nod to Graham, "Let's get your grandfather before the sky does."

15

Back at my place on the third floor and all the world melts away.

I sift through the mail piled on the floor beneath the mail slot. Bills. Credit card applications. An appeal letter from Saint Erasmus, the Catholic parish I attend on Christmas and Easter. Needs money. Father leads the flock there. A good man. He's done right by me.

I sit back and take a breather. Later tonight Graham wants to meet up at his grandfathers and drink a few beers to his grandmother. Fine by me. Graham said he was even going to make his famous dip. I'll pass on that.

Weariness lays its hands on my shoulders in a gentle massage, and I lean my head back, close my eyes and exhale long. Every muscle in my body feels strained from the past few days. Just sitting in a car for hours has a toll. The numerous brands of tension borne from hunting people, the loss I absorb as I watch Clevenger fill with sorrow, the set of eyes in the back of my head as I do things like pick locks.

This much exhaustion just means I'm not drinking enough to cope. I open a bottle of whiskey and savor the initial burn. That's how you how you know it's working.

The smokehouse next door is hard at work getting tomorrow's meats ready. The stale but pleasant lingering scent of tobacco in my place surrounds me, envelopes me. The aroma of the booze fills my throat and nasal cavity with its sweet spice.

But still, a waft of gardenias trail through it all and with a loving embrace I have never found again, caresses my cheek and calls me to the bedroom. To the closet where I have kept my wife's belongings.

My beautiful wife, the only thing ever right with this world. Given unto the Great Hereafter, accepted with joyous blaring of trumpets and angels singing as she crossed untainted into the Kingdom of Heaven. How I ever won her I don't know, nor do I spend any time dwelling on it. I did win her. And that simple fact alone tells me there is a God, and He does not hate me the way I think He would. A more bitter man would accuse God of giving my wife only to take her away as a cruel joke; an example of how much the Divine truly does despise me. But I do not.

I know God cherishes my wife and would not use her as a joke against me. But moreover, He would not use *me* as a cruel joke against *her.*

And then Death herself, that filthy cunt who spreads her wings all around me, all at once a beautiful but insidious dame, she came and ran her poison through my wife's veins.

I open the closet and am bathed in the ethereal traces my wife has left behind. Her wedding ring, twinkling in the light of the closet bulb. The way the sunlight danced across her eyes when she would look at me, seeing something no one, even my mother, ever saw. I take the ring into my hardened fist and hold it tight. So tiny there. Sometimes I can feel her nimble fingers explore the creases in my palm. I close my eyes.

Four days.

Four days between the wedding mass and her death. Four days personified as gently strolling poetry, scene after scene of her happiest days passing by like silk in the wind. Behind each simple glory there was a stain of death to be sure, but each stain was *behind* her joy. That much she was thankful for.

She knew the blip at the end was coming; even before she said "I do" she had been to her MOPP regimen. After our first dance as man and wife she had to sit. Taxed beyond her limits. Stayed on the oxygen tank for the next three songs. Wheelchair bound for the rest to ease her burdens.

She was both alluring and complex. Blonde, warm like dawning sunlight across gold. High cheekbones, emeralds for eyes. She never struggled with people. They loved her. Everyone knows one person like that; the easy magnetism, the pretty girl looks with the ugly girl personality. Genuine. Magic. Approachable and disarming, unintimidating even though, if she so chose, she could be untouchable. Sometimes she would fall quiet as she contemplated a shift in the leaves on trees, but only if it were autumn and the colors rustled just right. It was her favorite season.

She never sang out loud because she said her voice was nasal in tone. *When the world has songbirds like Karen Carpenter and Donna Summers, they don't need crows like me.* But she would hum under her breath and stir the heartstrings of angels whose ears were delicate enough to listen. Tuned to her songs fit for God's reception. Both humble and captivating. Her smile was gummy yet exactly right. Her laugh sounded like it came straight from Rhode Island even though she'd never set foot on the East Coast. Yet it came with a warmth that dulled the percussive edges.

She was perfect and the fact that she would never know it made her more so.

At sixteen her leviathan surfaced. It went into remission when she was seventeen. It came back when she was barely twenty-one. She was called home at twenty-one years, ten months, twelve days and almost one hour.

But no matter how hard her disease tried to hollow out her flesh and leave her empty, her beauty persisted. Yes, her collarbones were more prominent than sins on a murderer;

every bone and joint seemed to be lightly painted with skin instead of covered by it. Yes, her shoulder blades became ungainly and withered wings of crudely hewn stone under her flesh. Yes, the cords in her neck constricted and cut deep lines through her throat every time she coughed. Hurt like hell.

She cried so much out of agony. She couldn't sleep most nights because of her suffering. But her beauty persisted. Her artistry.

Human beings wear their atrocities on their sleeves. One only needs the proper set of eyes to read the fabric, to decipher the horrors committed and woven in. I thank God those same eyes could also see her enchantment, floating like candles on a storm surge, never winking out, never getting so wet as to extinguish, only persisting. Persevering. Her beauty. Her artistry.

It all came from the inside. From a well of *calme beauté* and understated brilliance that arrived with her from the heavens. Meeting her proved that somewhere there is a God. There must be. It is the only explanation of her. Her beauty. Her artistry.

No ravenous affliction can rot that out. Even though near death, even *through* actual death, a gorgeous soul will radiate. Through the bitter thorns, through the melancholy, through the wasting.

Hers did.

And those four days, we were married a lifetime.

With her I buried any reason to live. Any compassion. Any withholdings. And that's okay.

I don't need them anymore.

16

1030 hours, Wednesday

My business line rings.

I let the machine answer it. I killed that booze in a half hour. Mostly passed out on the couch, empty bottle fallen from my hand and long ago rolled across the wooden floor with a hollow note, I fight to keep my bleary eyes shut as a man whose voice I do not recognize speaks into my machine.

"Hello. This message is for Dick Buckner. I got your email."

I sit up.

"Mr. Petticoat doesn't have the balls to try and adjust our arrangement. Nor is he very thorough at hiding his tracks or even checking his rearview mirror to see if he's being followed while he goes to meet a washed-up cop. Anyways, short and sweet. I—"

I stand up to get the phone as the first runner of color zings down my vision. Big Fry smear. I shake my head violently to stop this but it only sends more runners down in a waterfall. Brown at first, the color of the wood beneath me, whiskey brown next as my stomach revolts. I taste the bile and booze as my vision constricts and I know I've vomited everywhere but it's no good. My knees come alive with pain. I must've fallen to them. My face next. The browns sink deep into black waters and my ears ring numb. I can barely breathe and the panic turns the black into a jiggling white. Pinks stream through it and I can hear the rapist from a million miles away talk in a cartoon voice as my brain seizes and melts, drains down my spine and spills out the bottoms of my feet. Then it crawls back up as the pinks turn to reds turn to oranges turn to yellows turn to greens turn to blues and hatred. So much hatred.

Then it all washes away, taking me with it.

I come to on the floor.

I hear the traffic outside. Spring birds. The cold wooden floor beneath me has warmed up considerably. I dread to think how long I've been lying here.

One eye cracks open and all it sees is mush. Ambient light is harsh, muddling. It's also taken on a bronze hue and I hope that is from blood and not dusk. I try and open the other eye but it feels huge. Swollen. Leave it alone then.

I slowly drag one hand up from my waist. Then the other. I exhale into the pool of sick mess around my mouth. I push up off the floor and peel my face from the drying vomit. My neck can't support my head's weight. I go up anyways. My chest hurts. My left side especially. The only times it feels like this is when I get drilled in the ribs. One hot, stabbing spot.

I crash back onto my ass, legs bent beneath me. Feel my face. Shiner over the eye. I manage a look at the clock nearby. Almost six p.m. Fuck. I work my way to my feet. Aches and pains, stiffness and atrophy burn and come alive with screeching alarm.

I walk to the machine. It flashes zero. I hit the PLAY button and get nothing.

You have no new messages. I hit it again. *You have no new messages You have no new messages You have no new messages You have no new messages You have no new messages*

I rub my face and go to the bathroom. Wash the stink off of me. I don't have hallucinations preceding a Big Fry smear. That shit happened. I got a phone call from the rapist.

Water running down my face, etching lines through my stubble, my eyes sore and dry and bulging from the whiskey, even my teeth feel gritty and ache. My stomach sour and vile, my shoulders twisted because I slept on them wrong, stuffed onto the couch. I get weary just cataloging my body's condition.

I remember flashes of the morning. Funeral. Then holding her picture. Holding her ring. Stumbling like I do when I drink to forget her as opposed to just drinking. Somehow I got on the couch. I remember trying the TV for a while. I remember lying with my head at one end and then later, with my head at the other end.

A wave of nausea percolates up from my twisted gut and I close the toilet lid. Sit down. The phone ringing climbs up from my memory like a rat clawing to the top of a sewer drain as it backs up. The ringing echoes. His voice comes across. He knows my name, although he commits the cardinal sin of calling me Dick.

No one calls me Dick. No one.

He got the email, he said. He tailed Petticoat. Then the smear. I sit. Wait for my stomach to back off. In the meantime, the sounds of the living world continue to sneak around corners and play out next to my ears. People down on the street, yapping as they live their lives and pass into and out of my own by walking on my sidewalk. Birds busy building nests on signs and ledges where there are no pigeon spikes to interrupt them. Taxis zooming around, surely speeding and nearly hitting pedestrians.

I hear my neighbor unlock his door. Slam it shut. Something different about it. Louder. More crisp. Jerry is an asshole and prone to being obnoxious and loud, but this is different.

I open my eyes, stare into the lightless bathroom. Tune an ear. Jerry's door opens again. His footfalls like explosions into the hallway. The wood floors and bare walls outside my doorstep magnify the sounds of his existence. He shuts his door, jangles keys into a lock. The deadbolt falls home and Jerry trots off. All too blaringly loud.

I uncover my face. Stand. Open the bathroom door. Walk into the front room and look. My door is open. Wide fucking open.

Someone came inside my place while I was there on the floor, unconscious, defenseless, destroyed and in a pool of my own vomit.

17

The front door lock has been picked, not kicked in, drilled out, blown up or anything else.

If the rapist was involved in a burglary and the late Detective Gillispie didn't find anything resembling forced entry, I figure he has more skills than just having sex with unwilling women. He came here.

I shut the door quietly and my mind begins to race on what I need to do. Search the house for missing items, bugs and bombs for sure. Send him another email and try to meet. Find out why he would call me, leave a message, then just come over here and erase it. What was in that message? Why come here and risk it? Better yet, why come here and leave me alive?

I walk to my wife's closet. Unmolested. My gun, still loaded and in the holster. For an hour I search the house. No bugs, no bombs. I feel the hot spot on my ribs and think he did kick me. I brew some coffee, take a shot of whiskey and go over to the answering machine. It's a long shot but I try and lift a finger-print from the ERASE button.

I get one and doubts immediately come to the surface. Might be my own. I fingerprint the outside door handle. Look for anything else disturbed. Nothing. He could very well have called, got the machine, left a message he immediately regretted, figured since he got the machine I wasn't home, raced over, picked the lock, came inside and saw me on the floor, erased the message and gloated while he kicked me on his way out. Left the door standing open as a taunt.

I brace the front door with a two by four. I walk into the bedroom and strip down. As I pull my shirt up over my head it leaves a wet trail up my neck onto my scalp. I examine it. Spit. I see red.

Did this fucking guy really loom over me, kick me and spit on me? Please, God, say he did. He already called me Dick. I have to breathe in and out in a slow, methodical manner to keep my steam from blowing like a nuke. I collect my wits, get a sample of the spit and keep it with the fingerprints.

I have to do something to vent. I punch a hole in the wall.

I shower. Smoke half a pack while I tear a sheet of paper into thin strips. Concentrate. Ruin something. Exercise my anger.

Finally I crush out a Rum Coast and open up the laptop. View Petticoat's email. Nothing new. Just like me, the rapist is trying to keep Petticoat in the dark about this. And why not? If Petticoat is still paying him his blackmail cash, why upset the apple cart with anything?

I email the rapist and write, "We should meet." Hit SEND.

Willibald and I sit on his front porch, the music of beer bottle caps popping off filling the night.

Graham is inside; stirring some horrible concoction he refers to as his "famous buffalo tuna dip." The red pepper sauce dances along the air through the living room, waving acrid tendrils along our nostrils. Mix that with the oil-canned tuna and I'm ready for another beer.

"Guess what I'm not eating," Willibald says.

"Graham will guilt me into one or two bites."

Willibald raises an eyebrow. "Oh, well then, guess what you'll be vomiting."

I laugh as Graham comes outside and waves around a bowl of red-tinted slop. "Get some, get some. I got the crackers, I got the pretzels, I got the cold beers, I got what you need."

"You got dysentery," Willibald says, pushing away the arm Graham is using to hold the dip. "Smells like you learned to cook in Southeast Asia."

Graham plops down into a chair, feigns being hurt. "I'll have you know this has won awards."

"I'll bet it has." Willibald looks at me and takes a bite out of a cracker. "Award for fastest shit storm ever."

"No, that's Richard here," Graham says.

"Don't involve me in your squabble. I came here for the booze."

"Hurry up and drink it then, Richard. We ain't got all night." Willibald hands me a second one and stares until I polish off my first. I crack open the new bottle and he looks away, satisfied that his houseguests are doing the master's bidding. "Hell, Richard. You take two. Ice that shiner."

I take a second one, and just like in those fancy commercials from the '90 s where one dude hands another dude a bottle of beer and the bottle is wet and the ice slides down the side and you can't think of anywhere you'd rather be, I get that beer. Lay it upside my swollen face. Heaven. Pure Heaven.

I look to Graham. He leans back to meet my eye line, his head appearing behind his grandfather's. He winks. Gives me a cheers salute. I return it and enjoy the silence.

"Nights like these came and went in the war, you know," Willibald says, his voice filling with that ashen tone that any grizzled veteran has when he remembers the times where killing was the only business at hand besides dying. "Little skirmishes, getting jumped I guess you boys would call it. They'd send a few guys here, a few guys there. They'd wait until the night had settled in just enough to have shadows for cover but not enough to where their muzzle flash would be a dead giveaway."

Willibald rubs his bottle across his forehead just as I imagine he did back in the war, taking his cap off and using the back of his hand to clear his brow. "So you had to balance the beautiful evening with the threat of bullets around every corner."

"Yeah, you're right," I say. "It was warfare. Demoralize your enemy."

"It solidified us," Willibald says. "When God gives you an evening like this, you can't help but see His hand in it. How the insect song slowly crescendos for hours in synch with the failing light, tuning up just a bit as it tunes out. How the breeze pushes through the tree branches and flutters them in a lullaby. And those sonsabitches would sneak in and shatter it like a jaw in a street fight."

Graham snickers. "I hear that wasn't the only bad thing about the Nazis."

Willibald laughs. "Yeah, but it might have been the worst thing, though."

"Yeah," Graham says.

"Did your grandmother ever eat this fish mush?" Willibald holds the dip in one hand, slowly using a cracker to tease out a hunk of the award-winning buffalo tuna dip. Graham smiles and snorts, shakes his head as his grandfather mocks his centerpiece for the evening.

"I like to think Grandma would have loved it."

"Your grandmother loved fresh salmon and little else. Cajun tuna on a cracker would probably—"

I see Willibald holding the cracker, suspended in air as the first staccato blast cleaves the stillness. The cracker, in slow motion like everything truly agonizing, it explodes into tuna splatters and grain dust as bullets cut through everything.

The dish explodes into millions of cheap white ceramic shards. A glob of Frank's Red Hot and a can of tuna spray outward like a bad prank. I can't see Willibald's hand and I can't see his smile as he toys with the food and all I can hear are the *pop pop pop* of projectiles punching through the windows and siding behind us.

Graham turns red and falls or dives I can't tell and I feel the hellish sting of a round zip an inch or less off of my forehead. I drop, grabbing Willibald's pants and yanking. Get him down, shield him. I can't even look up I'm covered in that tuna dip and all I hear are screeching tires.

Adrenaline. Every sound pinches down to a mosquito squeal and I feel my heartbeat thudding. Pieces of the wood deck splintering and flying about. I dive to the old man and his grandson. Just like in the war. Hot lead speaks a language all its own, but still somehow everyone who hears it understands it plainly.

I get a split second where the whites of the shooter's eyes meet my own. I see his face just enough to feel secure in the fact that the next time I see it I'll be beating to death the right coward. The facial hair, the baby cheeks and high eyebrows. Ugly.

"Willibald! Stay down!" I'm on my feet, .44 Magnum out and rushing into the yard. A car screams down the road and takes a corner on two wheels.

I charge with everything I have. Across the street. Through the neighbor's yard. Up and over the fence, rattling like ten thousand scales on a knight's chainmail as I vault it. Hit the ground in a flowerbed. Trample. Rush forward; dodge a pooch that comes yapping at me after bolting from its doghouse. Over the other fence. Around the house and into the street.

Empty roads greet me. I spin around, hunting. Looking. Listening. Demanding the world to offer me a sound. A target. But as I turn, gun out, and that fresh adrenaline dump turns into burning gasoline in my veins and all of a sudden my lungs are only getting half the air they were a second ago and the sweat itches like steel wool down my scalp and my shoes are wet from God knows what and my suspenders are too loose and my shirt is untucked and fuck it, fuck all of this. I stop spinning. Gone.

Gone. I think the car was brown. Looked old and long. Town car. Sedan. Four doors, maybe. Probably.

Deep breath while I stare down the street, and I don't feel the torch holes of bullet wounds. I holster and wipe off tuna dip from my shirt, my pants. My face. That fish slop burns worse than the sizzle of getting grazed by a round.

I walk up the street, turn the corner. Take my jacket off and snap it, trying to work out the wrinkles. I get a few houses down and jog over to Willibald's. Off in the distance I hear sirens playing our music.

Up the steps onto the porch. Graham. Crying. On his knees, back and forth, rocking. Holding Willibald. And all that red everywhere.

I kneel down, put an arm around Graham. I watch the street for more of the gangbanger turds, and I feel Graham's hand climb up and grab my arm. Squeeze so tight he might think if he lets go he's going to float off.

"I'm feeling petty," Graham says in a voice I've never heard him use before.

"I do too, and this is war," I say, and I hold my friend while his grandfather goes off to join his wife now that his circle is complete.

18

Seven a.m., Thursday

My stomach is sour from lack of sleep.

SAPD processed that scene well into the night, Graham and I being fed cups of burnt, black coffee as we gave our statements over and over. They wouldn't let Molly through the police tape. Made her wait, sobbing and alone on the other side until Graham walked off mid-sentence, took his wife in his arms and came back with her.

The gang unit's ears were to the ground the moment the 9-1-1 call came out. They heard one thing. Thuggie himself pulled that trigger.

I go to a greasy spoon and sit at the counter, rub the bridge of my nose. Ponder how exactly those turds went from me at Moss's to this. But that lone dude at Eudora's funeral, studying faces, he keeps coming back to my mind.

Abe Baldwin: my main man. He failed himself, his overbearing mother and the community at large with how terrible he was at being an assistant district attorney. Now he practices privately and sends clients my way. I dial is number. It's seven in the morning, so no doubt he's swaddled in a towel, the youngest man by thirty years sitting in a sauna over at the country club up north in Gravel County.

He always has his cellular leash on him, in case his never-gonna-die mother or his needs-to-die-tomorrow wife calls. He answers before the second ring expires.

"Hello?"

"Morning, Abe. Taking a steam?"

"It's seven in the morning, isn't it?"

"Sure. I need something."

"Speak, my friend."

"You remember that shit bird gangbanger you defended on the weapons charge?"

"Buster Ford? Great kid," Abe says and I can hear the smile on his face. That's one of the reasons why Abe was so terrible at being an ADA. Abe only sees the good in people, even when they're standing before him covered in blood and carrying the severed head of their latest victim. Although, that trait worked out well for his wife. No one else would have married such a troll.

Buster is not a great kid. He might be keeping his nose relatively clean now, but that's only because he's had to flee the city lest he be gutted and eaten in front of his family.

Buster was known to the gang world as Raptor. Now he's known as Snitch. Apparently in his Raptor days he was one mean motherfucker. He'd been in the clink twice, almost right in a row. He was imprisoned on a count of aggravated battery against a law enforcement officer, released on parole and put right back in on a domestic violence charge for putting his brother through a wall.

Buster got out a second time and was pulled over by a patrolman for running a red light. In plain sight, lying across the back seat of the car were two AK-47 knock-offs Buster was delivering to a rival gang. Seems intelligence and loyalties were lost on him.

Buster knew if this hit the light of day or worse, if he went back in the pen, both his ass virginity and his life would be taken from him faster than he could say "plea bargain." Abe was his court-appointed lawyer. Buster turned state's evidence bigger than shit to make sure he got parole instead of hard time.

He now lives in Three Mile High working at a yuppie sports bar where they serve beer and specialize in chicken wings. Buster and his ankle bracelet monitor are cautiously avoiding anything that resembles Saint Ansgar nowadays.

"I need to meet with Buster," I say.

"How about a phone call? I'm fairly certain I can get him to agree—"

"No. Face to face. Here, in the city. Today. Tell him if he says yes we'll meet on his terms. If he says no, we meet on *my* terms."

I crack the knuckles on one hand. "He'll want to say yes."

"Let me see what I can do," Abe says.

"We can meet somewhere right off of the rail line so he's not too inconvenienced. He's not getting any money or favors. What I'll do in return is not sell him out to the two gangs he screwed or the six bangers who got hard time over his testimony."

Abe laughs. Again, with some mirth this time: "Let me see what I can do."

"Thanks."

Abe calls while I'm driving.

That shitbag Buster Ford can meet after dinner at the Cake Hole, a donut shop a block off of the rail. Fine.

"Buster wants you to bring him a gift," Abe says.

"I'll think of something," I say. I hang up, immediately see what I'm looking for and pull off into a strip mall parking lot. I walk into a low-rent hip-hop clothing store. Above the door in colorful, graffiti-influenced script a sign reads: Saint Ansgar Phat Urban Styles. So be it. The few patrons and the clerk eyeball me as I come inside. I sift through the racks and pull out my phone.

The clerk steps over to a spot at the counter that effectively shields his waist and hands from me. He keeps looking down at the glass-top counter and the items inside on display as if that's fooling me at all. With his head tilted down, his eyes continue to roll up, snatching glances my way. Maybe he saw my iron under the jacket. Might be a bulge. Even with my wingspan it's hard to tuck a large frame Magnum caliber revolver into a shoulder holster. Oh well.

If he gives some kind of signal to the other patrons then I'll know it's time to take aim and back out of the store slowly. I turn one eye to the clerk. He knows I'm watching him.

A patron stops browsing and walks towards the door. He shoots eyeball glances to the clerk. The more I think about how that guy was looking at merchandise the more I think he wasn't looking at all. As if he knows the racks inside and out because he's been studying them for hours and hours while he waits for a guy like me—a guy who don't belong in these parts—to come inside and shop.

As he walks to the door he's got his left hand holding his pants up. As he browsed he was using his right hand to shift through the clothing. I'm guessing that's his dominant hand. He might need to hold his pants up because the goddamn things are strung so low his belt is cinched around the knees. Or it might be because tucked away inside there is a firearm he'll want to grab with his dominant hand.

When the time comes. Which, my piggy sense tells me, is coming fast.

Another patron steps off the floor and through a backdoor. Gone. I look around openly. It's now just the clerk, the doorman and I. Doorman moving to my back. The clerk waiting for me to walk up to buy something.

I select a T-shirt. Look out to the street. The road outside is busy enough with daytime traffic that, in this part of town, only looks ahead. Some of that is because there is nothing of value to look at roadside unless iron bars, graffiti and the homeless are captivating.

The other reason no one looks around is because, quite simply, they don't want to see what's happening.

I walk to the counter. Toss the T-Shirt on it. Look at the clerk, who has a barely perceptible sheen of sweat across his brow. His eyes go from me to the door. Me to the door. He doesn't notice it but he shifts his weight from one foot to the next, back and forth. Nerves. Maybe he's new to the game. Maybe the last time they did this it went south. Maybe he doesn't want me to be the target. Let me see what I can do to further that notion.

"I see the price tag says fifteen bucks," I say. "I'd like to make a deal with you."

"No deal, bro," the clerk says. "Fifteen dollars is fifteen dollars. Plus tax. Then you leave."

"Hold on, now. How about I walk away with the T-shirt and in exchange for that, I don't disarm your friend at the door and beat him ugly with his own gun. Sound good?"

"Price just went up to twenty. Pay up or get out." His voice trembles in a way that most folks wouldn't pick up. This kid is nervous, but barely. What he wants is for me to go to the door. The doorman must be the alpha male here. Probably why, in this little strong-arm racket these punks are running, he's the doorman. He must be the stone cold one. The clerk here, he's a tagalong.

"Okay." I leave the shirt on the counter and walk towards the entrance. The doorman is nowhere to be found. I step outside and as soon as I do a voice from behind me says, "Hands out. Go back in."

I stop. My hands go out. The traffic across the street has a red light. My car is twenty feet away. I don't move to go back in and I hear the doorman step forward. One big, close-the-gap step. The gun touches my back just enough to say hello and then disappears. Doorman steps away. Opens up. Out of reach.

"Folks down here know better than to get involved," he says. "You shout for help, I hit you. You wave your arms, I hit you. You waste more time out here, I hit you. Getting hit with a gun hurts, bitch."

Tell me about it.

"Now, what you're gonna do is what I told you to do. Turn around, and go back inside. If we stay out here any longer, I'm gonna get mad."

"Okay."

I turn around to the front door and walk very slowly. I'm sure the doorman thinks I'm scared shitless. And while he's thinking he's got the upper hand, smiling like a self-gratified idiot, I'm studying him in the reflection, moving at a crawl towards where I'm going to teach him a lesson about fucking with me.

He's got a grill. Loose, extra-long shirt and pants so baggy there's more fabric piling up on his shoes than anywhere else. He's holding a beefy semi-auto in his right hand, left hand still on those damn ridiculous pants. Finger on the trigger, gun canted thug-style.

The door opens inward. I look at the clerk. Still at the counter. He peers over my shoulder at the doorman and smiles. My left hand still on the door as I step in past it. The clerk looks to me. I wink.

Blast off.

Swing the door as hard as I can and the doorman either has to get clocked by it, drop his pants to catch it with his left hand or take the gun off of me to catch it with his right. Right hand dominant. He reaches with the gun hand to stop the thing. And I turn around. One hand clamps the gun and hand together. The other hand peels that trigger finger back with a crisp *snap*. I take one huge step inside. Right hook to his glass jaw and that fucking grill flies out of his mouth and sails across the room, trailing saliva and fresh blood. Snatch the semi-auto from his paw and swing. Right between the eyes. Once, twice, three times. I get up to six and then grab him by his unconscious neck and hurl him at the register.

The clerk dives for something. The doorman crashes into the

counter and crumbles down. I get to it, look over the top. See the clerk's foot-long braids as he's down on one knee digging for something. Grab a handful of his hair. Pull. Squeals as he launches up and over. He comes with me at a sprint across the room. Feet dragging, arms uselessly flailing, forehead predestined to kiss the stud behind the drywall. *Kaboom.* Wall, meet face. He drops to his knees and keels over to the side. Hard. The head-sized crevice in the dry wall has a comical wet red dot in the middle.

I walk to the back wall, stand next to the door the third dude disappeared into. I breathe deep and try and calm the rage setting me on fire. *They're just punks running a scam in a part of town where this shit sometimes happens. Don't kill anybody. Give them some help.* Give them some help, as Clevenger and I used to say. Count to seven before the door opens. The third dude steps into the fray, muzzle first. He never sees me. Just my bare knuckles swinging a haymaker at his nose. A satisfying *crunch* and lights out.

The guy is armed with another semi-auto. I take it. I take the doorman's piece as well. A quick glance behind the counter and see a sawed off shotgun the clerk was trying to dig out. Two more seconds at best and he would have had it pointed at little ol' RDB. Mine, now. One can never have too many drop-guns. For as much as I love my .44, I don't want its bullets getting traced back to me.

The T-shirt is on the counter. It joins me as we go outside. Guns in the seat next to me, shirt on top. I leave. Think about where I'm going to have lunch.

19

1804 hours

The Cake Hole.

The Cake Hole is a donut shop on the platform with enough seating for twenty people or so. It's reminiscent of an airport food court place. I bet this shop makes a killing around the morning commute. The commuter rail train between Three Mile High and Saint Ansgar arrived at 1802 hours by the official rail platform clock. Buster should be on his way here.

In one hand I have Buster's T-shirt neatly folded into a wad with a piece of Scotch tape wrapped around it. In the other hand I have a printout of his mug shot from the county jail's website. I study the picture; look up into the crowd as it disgorges. Human cattle all mooing in unison as they do their zombie walk towards the parking lot.

Cutting through the crowd comes Buster. He's wearing a long sleeve jean jacket unbuttoned. It's three sizes too big. Better to hide a firearm that way. His matching pants sag. His belt buckle is an absurdly large oval with a marijuana leaf on it. The buckle is big enough to serve as a sheath for a palm dagger. He's got the waist of his pants buckled mid-thigh.

He walks with the pimp limp. In his mug shot he has corn-rows and an unkempt, patchy beard. Now his head is shaved clean and he has a mustache with some kind of beard hair art. Meticulous.

Buster walks up. No hesitation. Looks me up and down. Sets his jaw off to one side in that thug tough guy look. He just his chin out and nods his head in one quick fashion.

"What's up," he says. "You Buckner?"

"Yes. And you must be Buster."

"They call me Raptor. You can too."

"They call you Snitch, but if you prefer Raptor I'll go the extra mile for you."

"Yeah. Do that. I'll call you Dick."

"You'll call me Dick once."

Buster smirks but he must tell from the sound of my voice I'm serious. "All right. I get it." He looks around. "So what's up? My train leaves in eight minutes."

"I brought you the gift Abe said you wanted." I hand him the wad.

He smirks again and opens it up. Reads the T-shirt. In the donut shop, in front of a crowd of dulled mid-level management, cubicle dwellers and people who need things like Friday night poker games with nickel buy-ins to bring excitement to their lives, Buster, a guy who couldn't look more gangbanger if he tried, looks at a shirt which reads SNITCHES WIND UP IN DITCHES. Standing in front of me, a guy who couldn't look more rogue cop if he tried.

"I hope you like it," I say. "I went through a lot of trouble to get that shirt."

"I bet you did. Anyways, I meant cash."

"This is better than cash," I say. "I got it from a store in a strip mall off of MLK Boulevard and Seventeenth."

"Phat Urban?"

"Yeah. That's the one."

"Shit. I hope not." Buster shakes his head dismissively. "I hope it wasn't Phat Urban. They hustle fools like you. Straight up rob."

"I doubt they will anymore."

"What's that mean?" His eyes keep darting to the Official

Rail Station Clock. Seven minutes until he thinks his train is leaving.

"Change of subject," I say. "Tell me about the Carnivore Messiahs. Specifically a guy named LaTrell they call Thuggie."

"No." Firm. "I ain't snitchin' on the mother fuckin' Carnivores. No."

"Listen to me. Over the weekend, members of the Carnivore Messiahs did a drive-by on the wrong house. They killed the grandmother of a cop—"

"Yeah." Buster interrupts. I despise that. "They blasted some old white woman. Tryin' to cap some guy called Green Fro. I live in Three Mile and I know that shit."

Andre Moss. Green Fro. I get it.

"Yup. Now this Fro goofball is dead."

"Yeah. They get it right." Six minutes.

"The gunman is dead. His buddies in the car were arrested."

"So you don't need me. Later."

He turns and I catch him by the shoulder. Yank him back. Gun barrel to his sternum. We're so tightly pressed together I can smell his sour breath. People looking at us might think we're embracing. He tries to shrug away. I mash the gun in more.

"I'm through fucking with you," I say, close enough for the heat from my breath to dry out his eyes. "You've got no problems selling your friends up the river to save your own ass. Now you'll do it to these guys or I'll go right back to the Phat Urban store and tell them I took that shirt for you as payment for information you gave me about the Carnivore Messiahs."

"You *did* do that—"

"Yes, Captain Obvious, I did. But the difference here is I wasn't planning on *telling* them that. But now, I'll just stuff you inside the rail—which doesn't stop between here and Three Mile High—and speed back to the store. Think I'll get there first? I do. I'll walk in, kill one of them, announce to the world it was all for you, the known snitch."

His eyes begin to register what it is I'm saying.

"Of course, I'll be sure to tell them you live in Three Mile High and work at that chicken shack. Shit, Phat Urban will tell somebody who will tell somebody who will tell somebody in the Carnivores. Does that gang have a set in Three Mile High? How far you think you'll make it before they find you? Do you think they'll just execute you in some alley, or do you think they'll take the Mexican approach and stuff you in an oil drum and set you on fire?"

Buster stares at me for a second. That second stretches out into an ugly eternity as he calculates what he thinks he can do. A lot of gangs branch out like chain restaurants. The chains are called sets. I'm sure there are a few goofballs up in Three Mile High who think they're Carnivore Messiahs. They'll be more than happy to wait on the platform as Buster gets off there.

"What you want?" he asks. Eyeballs the Official Rail Station Clock. Four minutes.

"Info."

"Look. Thuggie just rose up out of the ashes from the 'hood. Word is that one day, back when he was just a punk named LaTrell, a high-rankin' member of a Crip set just walked up to him to start a fight. I forget what they say about the Crip 'cept he was known for just fuckin' up fools. Just found some guy, rival gang or not, and threw down. But that day he walked up to Thuggie, got in his space, and wanted to brawl. And Thuggie straight up just jacked the dude right then and there in the throat with a knife. The Crip never saw it comin'. One second he's picking a fight with some stranger, next second he's stabbed in his neck. Dead.

"Word is that Crip's name was Thuggie. And when LaTrell found out his name, he took it as his own. Just to show everybody what's what. And he does shit like that. No one love him, not even his mama. No one like him, not even his mama. Everybody fear him, including his mama.

"I heard from people that Green Fro hustled an old woman

walkin' through his streets. Bitch was mindin' her own business. But then Green Fro come up and says he's disrespected 'cuz he ain't know who this bitch is so she must be new. And new blood on the street pay him for protection. So he rob her. Took her purse, her rings, earrings and some pearl necklace that meant the world to her. Done deal. Turns out the woman is Thuggie's grandma or aunt or some shit. She tells the family and word gets to Thuggie. Thuggie gets Green Fro's address, tells some of his new boys to go earn they way into the gang, they fuck it up and blast the wrong bitch, they go hit the right house and now whatever you said. They dead or arrested or whatever."

He shrugs away and I let him. Hide the gun before someone else sees it.

"That's what I know."

"Fine," I say. Crack my neck. "Where can I find Thuggie?"

"Don't know. For real."

"Where is their territory?"

"All over. They got 'hood off of Pinnacle Avenue all the way over to the piers."

One minute.

"Whatever you do," he says, "stay away from the corner of Baltimore and Forty-second. They own that."

"Why?"

"It's a four way stop. Everybody knows not to stop there. Just run the sign. If you stop, they have a car that comes outta nowhere. Blocks the road so you can't go. A dude comes to the window and jacks your shit. Try walkin' home in that 'hood. You wind up in the bay."

He starts to walk towards the rail. I call after him: "Baltimore and Forty-second?"

He barely looks over his shoulder and says, "Yeah."

Looks like I'll get carjacked in the very near future.

20

I call Graham, no answer.

All right. Molly then.

"Hello, Richard," she says, and I can hear the weariness in her voice. Normally her voice is bright, bordering on a little too loud, like that person in a restaurant who tries too hard to be heard over the low-level din. But not now. She's soft. Spent.

"Hey, Molly. I called Graham. No answer."

"He's sleeping. The doctor prescribed something to help."

I rub my face, inhale and exhale through my nose. On Molly's end I must sound like a snorting racehorse. "It'd be hard. I know I don't like it and they're not my grandparents."

"You're his best friend," Molly says, consoling me for something I haven't said yet.

So I say it now. "Willibald is my fault."

"No."

I nod. "Yes. Yes he is." Something else I don't want to say. "And Graham knows it."

"Richard, it's hard enough around here without you calling up to take ownership of all our problems." Molly is louder now. She starts crying. "When Graham needs somebody he calls you, most times before he calls me. And as a wife I'm not down with that but I so put up with it. I know what you mean to him. I put up with it because of what you mean to me. So don't start."

I want to tell her they must have been watching the obituaries until they saw Eudora's. The newspapers splashed her everywhere, and from there it's one plus one to find the funeral. I want to tell her when she and Graham and Willibald got into that stretched limo, that nine hundred foot black sign rolling down the road proudly displaying the grieving family, they must have been followed. And they were followed right back to the first crime scene. I want to say they did it because they wanted retaliation for my bullets at Moss's house.

But instead I just say, "I'm sorry. I won't start. How is Graham?"

"Oh, Richard," Molly says, quietly sobbing. "He's sleeping."

21

2138 hours

I keep a storage unit.

Not under *my* name, of course. There are too many illegal guns inside it for me to do that. I really don't do much else besides visit it two or three times a year. I pay in cash at the beginning of the year for the next twelve months. The storage company is both low rent and a shitty employer. Turnover there must be worse than an in-patient, budget psychiatric care facility. There's only so much shit one can take when one is being paid minimum wage to babysit adults who either scream constantly, live outside of reality or do nothing but drool and break incontinence records the globe over. My friend Jeremiah Cross knows a thing or two about that.

Suffice it to say I have never seen the same employee twice. As far as I know they could be pocketing my cash. But as long as they write me down as PAID I don't care.

Every now and then criminals have a good idea, and they do this once in a while. I've seen dudes use them as a meth-cooking house, someplace to stash stolen goods until they cool down. Clevenger told me about a killer who kept two bodies in an unplugged deep freezer inside a unit half the size of mine. The number of MacGyvers out there who just put the focus on the wrong thing...

I mostly keep guns in mine.

The name mine is under belongs to some dirt ball that I know to be very dead. The rest of the world might still think he's out there kicking around. Actually, I really hope so. Because if the place was ever found it's my sincerest hope the cops go looking for him. The guy had a couple of weapons charges on his record and he associated with folks who used guns, so it all looks like a good enough red herring. I guess.

I make deposits and withdrawals from the unit in heaps. I wipe down anything that goes inside the unit to make sure there are no fingerprints whatsoever, let alone mine. After the wipe down I wear gloves until the transaction is complete. I canvas the area thoroughly before I go inside. Then, it's all get in, get out.

Tonight I go. Key in the lock. Slide the door up. Rummage for a moment. Get the stuff; drop off the weapons from Moss's and Phat Urban. Leave. Time to finish the prep work if I'm going to get carjacked tonight. Excited that I get to shoot a fully automatic weapon.

22

0127 hours, Friday morning

I don't want to do this in my own car.

I listen to the police scanner for nearly an hour while I double, triple and quadruple check my gear. Finally, a noise complaint worth perking my ears over. Four calls altogether of various neighbors saying there's a party next door that is too loud. Too much ruckus. Too many people. I know the neighborhood they're talking about. The cops can stop by and say something but it will do no good. If SAPD does anything besides drive by and be seen I'll be blown away. The neighborhood is south of the river and rough like a poor Mexican town on a drug trafficking route. Police presence will not bring control. It's only punks looking to make names for themselves by fucking with cops.

I go there. Circle the neighborhood twice, making a selection. Sure enough, a house party is lighting up the whole block. Hip hop blasting. Beers. Smell the ditch weed in the air. Obnoxious laughter. Loud chatter competing with louder chatter, all peppered with vulgarities, big words used incorrectly and the occasional bottle being broken.

Park down the street, facing away. The car I want is three behind me. The house party is good camouflage. No one will notice my car in a sea of cars. Four more wheels and rust added to the mountain range of hoods, cabs and trunks that create a subtle crest and trough between the street and the ramshackle homes. No one will notice the car I'm stealing until I return it. Bullet holes and all.

Slim Jim inside. Lucky for me the steering column is already broken off. I hotwire it in under ten seconds. Bag of tricks beside me, my new sled and I ease out into the street. Half a block down I turn on the lights. I spark a Rum Coast cigarette and get comfortable. The intersection of Baltimore and 42nd is twelve blocks south.

The area is perfect for this.

Baltimore Boulevard, like most boulevards in Saint Ansgar, runs north to south. It's miles long and on the west side of the city near the waterfront. From about 35th to 48th is all industrial park, in varying shades of use and disrepair.

Brick structures, industrial, broken windows, concrete steps leading up to concrete stoops. Graffitied stop signs, stolen street signs; empty metal poles standing watch over intersections with no names now. Urban decay.

I figure most people, when they find themselves in an industrial park that feels so quiet it can only be a set up, they either turn around and head back to the first place where they remember life or they gun it through. No stopping. So I stop at every intersection. Complete cessation of movement. Chin to shoulder, looking down both cross streets. I'm a model driver.

South on Baltimore I get to 40th. Hushed and still, not even the susurration of the waterfront wants to be heard here. At 41st I check my gear for the final time even though that's all I've been doing tonight. Crowd control-sized pepper spray cannon. Check. Silenced, fully automatic Glock 19 with a fifty round drum magazine and grip stock. Check.

Carjackers, come out, come out, wherever you are.

Baltimore Boulevard and 42nd street. I pull up to the intersection and slow down, stop. As soon as I do some old '80s sedan comes flying out of nowhere on my left. Slams to a stop right in front of me. The car is more of a boat, up on a lift kit with golden spoke rims. It blocks the entire intersection. I expected the windows to roll down and gun barrels to emerge, but they do not. Excellent. This is a firsthand example of complacency. By the time they get those windows down to shoot it'll be too late.

A lone thug comes strolling from a shadow, cigarette dangling from his lips. Turd has a pimp walk, extra-large jacket, flat-brimmed ball cap cocked off to the side. Early twenties. The mouthpiece for this shitshow.

Turd moves with the confidence that if anything starts to happen to him, the car will squash it. But, unless the fuck-faces inside that hooptie are willing to blow out those midnight-tinted windows in an effort to shoot me first, I'll be winning this evening.

I'm anxious to get this started. The smell of the rubbing alcohol and diesel fuel I brought with me inside is getting to my sinuses.

I position myself. Turd gets to the window, hands in pockets and leans over at the waist to talk. Thank you for offering your face. I start to roll the window down.

He says, "What's up?"

"What *is* up?" I ask as I raise the pepper spray cannon.

Blast off. A cone of aerosolized devil spit hoses this thug queef up and down his fuck-ugly face, fake diamond grill and all. The liquid hurt mask digs under his lids, crawls up through his nose to the back of his throat and layers the inside of his mouth thick enough to steal the breath from his soul. It's all fire and claws hugging his mug. He falls back and I've already got the Glock 19 tucked into my shoulder, aiming at the hooptie.

This isn't my car so I don't give a shit. I point the barrel at the windshield and press the trigger back. Bullets cough out and before the thugs inside the car get their windows rolled down they get showered in lead. I sweep the gun across the passenger side windows and then lower it to the doors for a pass. A ballet of shattering glass and rippling metal bring the car to life as the thing transforms from a hulk of the '80 s to a block of Swiss cheese. The chamber clicks empty and I drop the magazine. Load the second one. Exit the car. Charge the hooptie from behind; come up driver's side. Spray it. Yank the driver's side rear door open. Four dead.

I move. Turd is rolling around in the street. Exquisite torment. The spray awakens every alarm klaxon in the human body.

Indians—dots, not feathers—have weaponized the ghost chili. That's what I have here. It's no longer the hottest chili in the world, but it's hot enough to make an atheist beg God for relief as he shits himself empty and writhes in agony.

I brought a one-gallon jug of water. That's not nearly enough to alleviate the pain of standard pepper spray, let alone this new excursion, but splashes of water will be cruel teases that may coax out answers.

Grab the water. Grab Turd. Drag him off to a curb bathed in shadow. Splash water.

"Where is Thuggie?"

He cries.

"Answer me and you get some relief," I say and jiggle the gallon jug over his ear. "Where is Thuggie?"

"I don't know!" he screams through his teeth. His nostrils have become leaking faucets. Thick streamers of snot have gooed him from the upper lip down to the lower lip and have even touched the concrete. I look at this ghost chili spray and give it an approving nod. If it were a dude I'd buy it a stiff drink.

"So where is he?"

"Don't know! Water! Please motherfucker! Water!"

"Who does?"

"Candy! Candy knows!"

Splash. "Who is Candy?"

"Candy Man! He deals straight for Thuggie! He'll know! Gimme some water! Fuck!"

Another splash. "Where?"

"Over at the John Wayne Theater! Water!"

"I'll decide when you get more water. The John Wayne Theater? You mean the old Pinnacle Theater? At Fiftieth?"

"Yeah! Yeah! Please! This shit burns like fire! Water! I need water!"

Splash.

"What's he look like?"

"Dark glasses and he's always on the phone! That's it! That's all I know! Water!"

I give him a splash and then pour the rest of the gallon out next to his head.

"Get up."

I snatch him up onto his feet and march him over to the hooptie. I open the passenger side doors and swing him into the corpses of his friends. Get their blood on him. All over. Over to the driver's side. Same thing. When Turd is good and slick I push him off to the rear of the car where he immediately resumes his flailing and screaming for water.

I go to the car I came in. Put on the gloves I brought and yank the windshield free from the car. Toss it off to the side and forget about it. Grab the diesel and the rubbing alcohol. Pour the diesel all over the inside of the hooptie. Splash the alcohol around. Got the accelerant, got the long, slow burn. I light it up. With a tremendous *whoosh* the inside of the car turns to an oven. Flames lick at the sky. Everything I do now is backlight in snatches of orange and yellow.

I loom over Turd. Put the barrel of the Glock 19 to his head.

"You're the only survivor of this grand fuck-up. You're soaked in your buddies' blood and you don't have a scratch on you. Smell that? That's your friends burning. You just sold out one of Thuggie's top dogs. You better fucking run. Got me?"

"Water!" he says. I laugh and toss the pepper spray canister in the fire. Heat will pop it. I get inside the car. Drive off.

Gloves on, I strip the Glock 19 as I drive. The barrel goes out the window as I cross an overpass. Under it there is a stream fattened with winter snow runoff. I slow to a crawl as I pass a storm grate. The slide goes in it. I flick out the remaining rounds into the bag I have. Stop at a dumpster and drop the receiver in. Toss a few bags over it. Stop at another dumpster and put the fifty round drum magazines in it.

I drive by a homeless pile and toss the gloves their way. The first one who comes to and tries them on will be the lucky winner.

The spot I took the car from is newly occupied as I return to the house party. I sneak the car into a space down the block and walk to my car. Get in. The car I stole isn't too bad off; it needs a new windshield but that's about it.

Folks are about, hanging out. Walking here and there. A second house has opened for business with the party so there are now two porches lit up with music blaring, people mingling, clouds of smoke rising. A grill is going. I can smell something pretty tantalizing in the air.

It's not a party until someone starts a mass panic to the tune of gunshots. Muddy the waters. So as I put my car into drive and pull out onto the street, if for nothing else to be an asshole, I stick my .44 out the window and squeeze off two rounds into the sky.

Both house parties go apeshit. Poked hornet's nest. People scramble, cars peel out. I know guns are drawn and pointed at everything under the sun.

Now, if the car I stole is somehow attached to the Carnivore Messiah bloodbath, it'll be traced back to this ridiculous house party that I'm sure is filled with felons and other gang members. No one else treads through this particular neighborhood. No one here will talk. No reason.

And if it's not attached, oh well. Anyone who saw me arrive or leave will have their memories muddled by the mass exodus going on right now. Human cattle turning into a frenzied stampede, a million directions taken by a million fools all at once.

Overall, it's a good night.

23
Morning

I call Carla Gabler, lean back in my office chair and put my feet up.

The morning light spilling into the single room hasn't quite yet reached the opposite wall, but it's making a steady march towards it. Never ending, I guess.

"Hello?"

"Carla, it's Richard Buckner, the detective who was asking you about Mickey the other day. How are you?"

"Oh. I'm fine. Did something come up?"

"Yes. While you were in prison and Mickey was getting out, you said he talked about a big score."

"The one he disappeared after. Yes."

"Can you tell me anyone who might know anything about that? Anyone. Friends, family."

"His parents are both dead. He has a sister named Joann. She lives somewhere north of the river. We don't speak."

"Okay. What's Joann's last name? Cantu?"

"She married. It's something French. Starts with a P. I'm sorry. She never cared for me. Mickey said his little sister never cared for any girl he brought home, even when she was eight years old and he introduced his homecoming date."

"All right. Joann P-something French. Got it."

"She lives in a posh townhome. I know that. Her husband is

an accountant."

"All right. I appreciate your help."

"Anything else just let me know."

Hank Madison's words float up into my mind and bring with them that horrible Gyro taste. "There is one more thing, Carla."

"Yes?"

"When you were incarcerated, do you remember a guard by the name of Clarence Petticoat?"

She hums a monotonous, scratchy note while she thinks. I can imagine her eyes squinting, one hand running through her hair. Finally she says, "Yes, I think so."

"Do you remember anything about him in particular?"

"Just that he was one of the guards who was accused of fiddling with the inmates. He disappeared in that big house cleaning I told you about."

"Did Mickey ever talk about him?"

"No. Why? Is he involved in this?"

"His wife was the rape victim."

"Petticoat's *wife*?"

"Yes."

"What a sleaze. I couldn't believe the girls in prison would touch him, let alone that a woman would actually marry him. Did he have money? The girls in the prison who would talk about him weren't worth the STDs, I can tell you that."

"I bet not. Thanks, Carla." I start to say goodbye and I can hear trepidation in her voice. She's not done with the conversation but she doesn't want to continue it, either. She needs to hear one thing.

I say plainly, "Carla, I don't think Mickey raped anybody."

A sigh of relief as wide as the Pacific. Then, gushing, "I told you, Mr. Buckner. Mickey might have been a burglar but he was a decent man. He was lovable and caring. Anyone who knew him doesn't remember him for the crimes."

"I believe you."

Borne on hope now: "Do you know where he is?" The question is a fragile thing that floats gently between us. My answer sets fire to its wings. Goodbye, hope.

"I don't think he's alive, Carla."

"I see." Quiet. Very quiet now.

I don't know what else to say. Whenever I'd do a death notification to a family it was awkward. People I don't know, telling them something that wrecks their lives, then, well, just nothing. Some people went quiet and sat there motionless. Others went apeshit and flailed about, destroying things. I've seen fathers go back to sipping beer and channel surfing. I've seen mothers start cleaning and offer to make me a snack. One woman played a game of solitaire on her computer; another played piano for twenty minutes and then broke down into sobs and fell right off the bench. One guy dropped to the ground and started doing push-ups.

Telling someone that a person they love is eighty-sixed is an odd thing. Carla Gabler knew it somewhere in her heart. She might have convinced herself of it because that was the only reason she'd accept for him not waiting for her. I think she cries, but keeps it to herself. I stay on the line for a while but only because I can't bring myself to say *well, this has been fun but I need to take a shit* and hang up.

So this is how we stay.

Eventually, she says, "Thank you."

"Not a problem," I say. "Listen, I have to go but I'm going to find Joann and ask her about anything Mickey might have said prior to his disappearance."

"She's a bitch, Mr. Buckner," Carla says. Cuts right in. "That woman was born thinking she was better than her family and now that her frog husband has money, she lets everyone know it."

"Okay. Will she be receptive?"

"No. If you walk in there and say Mickey is accused of murder she'll think he did it."

"Any suggestions then?"

"Yes. Avoid her."

"Anything else?"

"Tell her...tell her you suspect he was *murdered* like you told me—" Tears now. Tears when she says that cold word. "—she might fill you in on what she knows, but you have to make it sound good. Like Mickey wasn't going to do anything bad. Okay?"

"Okay."

We say our goodbyes and hang up. Mickey might have been a decent man, but the people he associated with after getting released from prison are not.

I think it cost Mickey Cantu his life.

24

0800 hours

The sister wasn't hard to find.

Joann Cantu-Pierre. She's in the book. Address at a high-end townhome complex on the northern rim of the city. The address comes back to a Jean-Luc Basile Pierre, a high-end accountant. Sounds about right.

The house: a ridiculous edifice which screams *my penis is so small not even a solid gold Lamborghini will make up for it.* There must be eight thousand square inside the place with a lawn virtually too small to hold it. I think about parking on the street, but decide on the driveway. It could play host to a drive-in movie theater. My car isn't swank enough to be on the property, so the aesthetic is ruined. The douche in me is satisfied.

I exhale long and go over my plan one more time as I wait for an answer to the doorbell.

A woman finally answers the door, plainly annoyed to have to do so at seven a.m. She is without make-up and should not be. Her lusterless blonde hair is very short and cut to be styled, which it is not at this hour and instead looks like a bedhead halo accentuated by electric shocks and two-day-old gel. Puffy eyes. Thin lips. Deep lines running from her nose down to her chin like Meg Ryan.

"Hello, ma'am," I say, trying to sound soft. "My name is

Richard Buckner. I apologize for knocking so early but I am looking for Joann Cantu, the sister of Mickey Cantu."

"That's me," she grumbles at the mere mention of Mickey. I can see her winding up to tell me to fuck off.

"Ma'am, I was a former detective for the Saint Ansgar police and Mickey was working with me on a case. I—"

"You've seen Mickey?"

"No, ma'am. We were working together quite some time ago—"

"I was gonna say I haven't seen that wretch since he got out of prison in 1992."

"Like I said, he was helping us when he got out and I believe—"

Joann snarls, "I mean, seriously? Twenty years and no contact? Who does that?"

"Ma'am, I was saying—"

"An asshole, that's who. Mickey was the type of guy to come over to your house and ask how much everything cost. Not because he was without couth, no. Because he was doing the math in his head on how much he could hawk your stuff for. You know he sold our dead mother's diamond—"

"Joann, close it," I say. She stares at me with indignation.

"Some jackoff comes on my doorstep and orders me to shut up? Just who the hell do—"

"Mickey was helping us and someone found out. Someone bad." I stare right back at her. "And I think Mickey got hurt over it."

"What do you mean hurt? Is he dead?"

"I believe so, ma'am."

Inside.

Joann walks around numbly; as news of her estranged brother's probable murder sinks in like a slow stain. Her coffee is so beyond café quality I'm actively thinking of ways to drag this out so I can drink more. I've even fought the urge to spike it with whiskey when she turns her back. And people have been known to place bets on when I drink straight coffee it's such a rare occurrence.

Joann walks over to a box of tissues, draws one but doesn't use it. She appears bizarrely confused about shedding a tear. Carla made it seem like Joann hates her brother, and now to find out on a random day at a random time from a random stranger that said brother has met his blip, it has plunged mixed emotions into her still sleep-heavy heart. I just drink more coffee. The president doesn't drink joe this good.

"I'd like to see his body."

"We don't have it, ma'am. I have confirmation of his death by testimony only."

"Who killed him?" she asks, her voice trembling like just the right nerve was pinched.

"That's what I'm trying to find out."

"Do you think it's a mistake?" She's grappling with something here. Minutes before, she was calling him a wretch and getting ready to throw me off her porch for mentioning his name. Now, at the news of his death and the finality of all of it, she is looking for ways to make this not so. One always feels better about despising family when there is still time to make amends.

"No."

Finally Joann's heart makes its decision and she sobs very hard. Just explodes into a deluge like a Midwestern spring storm. She braces herself on her counter and her knees look weak. Very weak. I peer at my watch. After about thirty seconds I take one more swig and stand up. Walk over to her, coffee mug in hand. Her knees buckle as I approach and I catch her with one arm; ease her to the immaculate tile floor. She slides her back against some cabinets and holds a tissue to her face. I get the box and offer it.

With a meager "thank you" she takes it, sets it down beside

her like an old friend sharing a park bench. I refill my mug and stand near her, hoping she thinks I'm a kind and gentle soul. While she cries I look around her kitchen and see what a childless, married and excessive life looks like.

All original art. I get the feeling prints are as good as toilet paper here. The frames are more expensive than most prints. Small decorative touches like glass jars filled with garlic cloves and red pepper slices suspended in olive oil, a mason jar meticulously layered in baking ingredients that could be poured out, mixed and turned into brownies. Food as decoration.

But the real impressive sights are the kitchen gizmos. Joann, plopped on her ass and crying, all the things she didn't say to Mickey or the things she did say and now can't apologize for, they come rushing back and I'm looking at the one gallon food processor she has on the counter next to her automatic paper towel dispenser next to her electric tea kettle next to her hand soap warmer. And that's not all. That's the first countertop. She's got miles of granite top counters in here. There is no island counter top. There's an entire archipelago.

Her coffee maker isn't just any coffee maker. It probably cost more than my car and it's about the same size. I see a digital read out on the motherfucker and that just doesn't look right. It has a steaming pipe for milk and a separate attachment for espressos. Then the water machine. Filtered, purified, reverse-osmosis or some shit. Her coffee bean grinder also has a setting and a digital read-out.

There are some muffins under a thick glass lid on a Lazy Susan within reach. I snag one. Cranberry citrus. I eat two before she is finished enough to speak English.

"You said he worked for you?" she asks, face buried in her hands.

"Yes."

Tell her you suspect he was murdered. She might fill you in on what she knows, but you have to make it sound good. Like Mickey wasn't going to do anything bad, Carla said.

"Prison set him straight," I say. "He was going to help us catch some guys we'd been looking for. Guys we had tied to the rape of a woman who was unfortunate enough to come home during a burglary."

Between sobs. "Now that you mention it, I remember him talking about helping you."

What? "He did, huh?" I ask, tuning in much more carefully now.

"Yes. When he got out he said he was going to help a guy. I could have sworn he said CO but he must have been talking about you."

"He said he was going to help a CO? With a burglary?"

"Yes. He said it was all planned out. I didn't want to listen. I just...I just *told him to leave.*" Starts crying again.

I stand up as the dots start to connect. Well, I'll be damned.

25

"Petticoat, I'm going to kill you," I mumble low enough so Joann can't hear it but I have to say out loud because some small part of me hopes he hears it wherever he is.

No wonder he was so off from the very beginning. Why his bullshit story was flimsy. Why he was so nervous just talking to me and why, even though he thought he was doing a good job being discrete, the rapist was still able to brazenly tail him to my office.

The plot: Petticoat knew Carla at Happenstance, gets transferred to the all-male prison for porking the women—they didn't fire back then they just shuffled their people. Geographical cure. Petticoat knows about Mickey because of Carla so he strikes a deal with him: I'll take my wife out to dinner and you burglarize my house for whatever end Petticoat was trying to reach. It pays both. Mickey gets all the scratch and Petticoat gets whatever it is he wanted. Insurance fraud, something. Maybe he just hated his TV and his wife wouldn't let him buy a new one. But instead Petticoat comes home, gets attacked and his wife gets raped. Where is Mickey and how did the rapist get brought into the picture? The wife whacks herself and now Petticoat is left holding the bag for this whole stinking pile of shit. He gets rich in real estate, gets blackmailed by whoever actually raped his wife. He's not sick and dying but he can't squeal without the rapist revealing what he did all those years ago. The whole thing about Carla sleeping with Martins was bullshit. Petticoat was just trying to get me started on Mickey's trail without letting me know about his involvement. Of course he wants me to kill the rapist. The assassin part. That keeps his hands clean, gets rid of the blackmail and shuts off whatever valve is ready to spill over and tell about how bad he fucked up back in the day. His own wife.

But why the Monday deadline?

Petticoat is still traveling to Three Mile High. The blackmail price just went up. He might have a deal up there that he won't have the money for if he pays the rapist. Got to be it. This guy isn't that complex. Clarence T. Petticoat is far from a mastermind. He's little more than a used car salesman with a smidge of imagination.

Connect Mickey to the rapist. This is all about him now.

I start to walk out the door when I remember Joann is still here, sobbing. I stop and stand there, looking at myself in the reflection of a glass cabinet. My eyes crawl off of my own ugly mug and onto Joann. Here is a woman I do not know. One man connects her to a woman with whom I have spoken. Carla says that her dead boyfriend's sister is a bitch and an elitist who is ashamed of her roots. I can believe that. I don't know her roots, how she was raised, her parents or anything else. I came here with that prejudice. I wouldn't have seen Joann any other way.

Of course, I barely know Carla. What I do know is she is a felon, in love with the memory of a dead felon. I think I've seen a glimpse of her heart when she opened up about Mickey. She made no bones about who she was. One reason she hates Joann is because of how cruel she said Joann was towards her love. But maybe another is because both women come from the same place and Joann spent her life trying to get out of it while Carla never did. Roots.

I'm not ashamed of my roots, but they are shameful. There is a difference. No matter what Joann is outside of our little moment in time here—snobby, bitter, falsely affluent—what she is *now* is a broken woman. I can see the guilt on her face about how she treated Mickey. How she felt about him. There are secrets there, deep inside, that make her cry for more reasons than loss. Everyone has those. When you tell enough people their loved ones aren't coming back, aren't going to keep their promises, aren't going to be around to continue their annoying habits like leaving the toilet seat up or drinking milk from the carton, all of a sudden the family want nothing more than to see the toilet seat left up one more time.

People want people around. They want *their* people around. And sudden acts of life and death prevent that. Here I am, most of the pieces of my puzzle fall into place, and I leave a woman on the floor to bear that weight by herself after I had the biggest hand in putting it on her.

If Joann Cantu-Pierre were a man, I'd continue to walk out the door. Since she is not I turn around and lift her to her feet. I am easily three times her size and I wrap my arms around her. Pull her in. Gently hold the back of her bedhead halo and rest my cheek against her ear. She cries again. She lets it out. Whatever deep secrets she has in there she has harbored against her brother, whatever thoughts she would be ashamed of admitting to, they come out with her sobs. I do the work of holding her upright so she may concentrate on cleansing herself of the guilt.

We stay like this for as long as she needs.

26

After a time, Joann separates herself from me and leans on a barstool before she finally sits down.

"Thank you," she says as she looks away. She takes her coffee mug and sips from it. "Cold."

I grab the pot and offer it to her. She holds her mug out and I fill it up. I scratch my head and want a cigarette.

"Joann, did Mickey ever talk about anyone else?"

"At first I thought he was going to have Carla in on it, whatever it was you guys were going to do. But she was still in prison I guess."

"Yes, she was."

"No. He never said anything about—well, he used to steal things and sell them to some shop down town. But that's a stretch, I guess. I never knew of him working with anybody except Carla. Why?"

"Just trying to put together a case. Do you remember the shop?"

"No." She drinks her coffee and blows her nose. "Did he die recently? Why wait twenty-something years to investigate?"

"We didn't know where Mickey was. You know. He just up and vanished. I got a break just the other day that made the case hot again."

"Can you tell me more specifics?"

"Not at this time." I need to leave now. I look at my watch

135

and feign raising my eyebrows. "I apologize but I actually have to go. I have a few more places to get to this morning."

"Damn you, Mickey," she says, staring at her tiny fists. "Sometimes I wish we never..."

I stare, waiting. Whatever it is, I want to hear it. When she stops talking, she looks at me ashamed. Finally, I have to pry. "You wish you never what?"

She looks away. "Nothing."

"It might help."

"No it won't."

And that is it. Joann is too taxed form her sorrow to do or say much more. I thank her for the coffee, her time, the information; apologize for the terrible news, blah blah blah. She walks me to the door and limply apologizes for how bad she looks. I blow it off as a courtesy. She does look pretty bad though.

In my car, I call Carla Gabler.

"Hello?"

"Carla, it's Richard."

"Hi. How'd it go with Joann?"

"Fine. Listen, when Mickey used to sell his scores, Joann said he'd take it to a pawn shop south of the river. Which one?"

"Let me think." I can hear her drag off a cigarette. I hear Carla's granddaughter playing in the background, laughing that musical note that all little children have. "Joe & Barry's Family Pawn."

Joe & Barry's. Good enough. "Thanks, Carla."

I hang up. Drive to Petticoat's.

I don't call ahead of time. I drive up to the office and see his car nosed into a space. I nose in behind him until my bumper touches its ass. I sift through my console and find a roll of pennies. I make a fist around it, feel the weight, slam my door and head in.

His office door is locked, but I can hear him on the other side of it. He speaks low. I hear a woman giggle. Say something coy. It's nine in the morning and Petticoat is getting ready to part his secretary's knees.

I pick the lock, open the door.

27

0921 hours

"Give us a minute, will ya, honey?" I say.

Petticoat and his secretary explode away from each other in a desperate attempt to conceal whatever it is they both have hanging out. Petticoat leans at the waist and fiddles with his zipper as his pants are left open like Travolta's collar in the '70s.

His secretary, blonde, ten pounds past 'curvaceous,' sweet-looking, squeals and tucks a freckled boob into her shirt with one hand while the other is grabbing handfuls of her skirt and yanking down. All she accomplishes is pulling it down too far and de-pants-ing herself.

"Petticoat, ask the dame to go into your office and take her time fixing herself up."

They just look at each other and his eyes say it all it. He flicks his head at his door and she scoots off. The door shuts. I pull up a chair to the front of the secretary's desk, sit down, kick my feet up and light a smoke.

"You're one serious motherfucker," I say.

"Just what in the fuck do you think you're doing here, Buckner? Aren't you supposed to be out there getting results? I mean really—"

"Oh, I've gotten results." Pull my iron and cock the hammer back. Point it at his face. "Sit the fuck down and get ready to explain some things."

Petticoat turns white as pureblood neo-Nazi and drops right where he is. Lucky for him a corner of waist-high filing cabinet is there to catch him or else I really think he would have just fell flat-ass to the ground.

"I'll just rattle some things off here and you tell me when it's enough. You used to be a corrections officer at Happenstance. You meet Carla Gabler there and she tells you about Mickey Cantu. You get washed out of the all-women's prison and wind up meeting Mickey. Arrange with him to burglarize your place. Something happens and your wife gets raped instead. Fast forward to when you're rich and your face is plastered every-where about town. The rapist sees this and knows you'll never squeal so he blackmails you. You pay until the price goes up and then you hire me, give me some complete bullshit story and hope I deal with your blackmail problem for you in a very final way. Sound right?"

He just stares.

"I went to the hospital you said you were at. Worked my magic. You're not scheduled for surgery."

"All right. Maybe I told you wrong—" he starts.

I jump out of the chair. Come across the desk. He screams like a bitch and falls off the cabinet. Gun to his eyeball, hand on his throat. I hear him piss his pants.

"Okay! Okay! Okayokayokayokayokayokay! I lied! All right! I lied!"

"GIVE UP THE STORY!"

"I just hated being a CO! All right? All right?" He swallows hard around my grip and tears roll down his face, up the crest of my fingers and down into the troughs between them. He breathes deep and his jaw shudders.

"Before—I dabbled in real estate before my wife got sick. I mean, *really* sick. The bills, all that. She needed the hospital but I convinced her to stay out until I could get a job that had benefits and when I did we had to wait until they kicked in...she almost died but we weathered through the worst of it. I wanted to go back to real estate, but you know how—how it is. I was already in the corrections job, had a few years under my belt, the wife was touch and go for a while, then I was just...I dunno, stuck. I was used to the routine, the guys I worked with, everything. But I just knew if I could get back into it...but it's so damn expensive. The license, the testing fees, promotional materials, the cost of speculation. It goes on. I needed cash. Everything costs money, man. So I thought, an insurance scam would be perfect."

He wiggles and I let him go. For good measure I shove him hard enough to send him sprawling. Lower the gun. Stand up. Walk back over to my chair where my lit cigarette is burning a hole in his carpet. Pick it up, take a drag.

Petticoat stands there behind his desk, looking helpless. "I...I just started looking around at Happenstance. See who the burglary folks were. Which ones were solid. My grandpa always said, *no matter whatchoo do in life, ya gotta surround yerself wit solid peoples.* He'd always say that."

He fiddles with his loose belt for a second, then gives up with a frustrated yank. "So I looked for solid. Carla wasn't, but her boyfriend sounded like it. He was over at the men's prison and it just so happens I got transferred there. Big hustle and bustle. But, I met Mickey Cantu, told him I knew his gal at my last gig. Told him I took care of her, you know; all the usual. Kept her safe from the gym teacher dykes and all the crazies, snuck her goodies. All bullshit, sure, but still. Bought his goodwill, I guess.

"We made a deal. Simple. I take my wife out on a date from six p.m. to ten p.m. He has a four-hour window to rob my house empty. Anything I wanted to keep I moved somewhere else. He could have the TV, stereo, furniture, art. I didn't care. Insurance money. Plain and simple, simple, simple. Then we never see each other again. He agreed."

He leans against the wall and looks furious.

"I come home at ten fucking thirty and we get jumped. I

open the door and *BOOM* I get hit square in the face. Out cold. I come to and the first thing I see is my house...it's still full. Nothing is missing. I was so angry I completely missed my wife sobbing in the corner, two black eyes and blood coming from her crotch. I walked through half the house in a trance while she curled up into a ball. And I did come back to her, asked if she was all right, the only thing she could do was ask me why I went walking around the house like that? What did I know? We had an agreement. We had an agreement!"

He cries. Drops to his knees. Bares his teeth like he wants to devour every word coming out of his mouth.

"I never told her. I never said it was all my fault. All this...I never said anything. Not to the police, nobody. Talking to you, right here right now, this is the first time these things have ever been spoken aloud."

He makes a fist and hits the floor, over and over. Curls up himself.

"And when she *committed suicide* I hoped there was no God. Because if there is she'd go to Heaven just because of the raw deal she got. And if she went to Heaven, she'd know what I did to her and what I hid from her. And, I guess she'd know about all the inmates I'd fuck while she was too sick and she'd know she completely threw her life away by ever setting eyes on me."

All true.

"So I wanted Mickey Cantu dead. But I'm no good at man hunting and I never found him. I don't know how hard I tried; the sick ironic thing is I had a life insurance policy on Sheila and when she died, it paid off. I had the money to get into the business then."

I don't know how hard I tried. Read: I asked around at a couple of bars and then bought a whore and stayed drunk for two months. *That's good enough, right?*

Petticoat smirks at the hideous fulfillment of his scheme. Not what he wanted, but the double-edged sword of the deal he made nonetheless cuts both ways. It took with one side, and gave with the other.

"Then all these years later, just like you said, I get an email out of the blue blackmailing me about that night. I paid because I didn't know what else to do. I couldn't call the cops, you know? Then the amount went way up. I needed help. And I remembered all those years ago working in the pen everybody there was afraid of you. The guys you put away, they'd wear a brave face but you get to know what fear looks like working in a prison. They'd talk about how rough you were. Some considered themselves lucky you were on the PD's leash. They didn't talk about what would have happened if they crossed your path and you were...a free agent, so to speak."

"So you look me up and see that now I *am* a free agent?"

"Yes. It was a no-brainer."

Again, all true.

"Ease yourself," I say to him. "Mickey Cantu is dead. My guess is he got a third party involved in your house deal. He would have needed another hand with Carla still locked up and all that loot to take. Whoever he teamed up with must have killed him and made plans to rape your wife instead. Explains why you got home a half-hour late and he's still waiting for you. *That's* the guy we want. He's preying on the fact that you still think it's Mickey Cantu. He gets away scot-free and a dead guy takes the rap."

"So we just tell him we're onto him, right?"

"No. Absolutely not. That's our upper hand. His guard is up anyways, but once he finds out we're sniffing for him instead of Mickey Cantu, he'll disappear. He's too smart and too patient. Way too patient."

"What then?"

"You meet him at the normal time and place, like he thinks you will. I'll take it from there. Now, tell me about the meet."

"Simple, really. I go to the bench at the northwestern corner of Macken Park and throw away a fast food bag into the trash bin there. Money's in the bag. I go about a hundred feet away and pretend like I'm watching the geese on the pond for five minutes. I assume that he comes by and grabs the bag then. I never see him waiting for me to drop it off. I couldn't describe him if my life depended on it."

I roll my head on my neck. "I'll think of something."

Petticoat raises an eyebrow and gives me a half-smile. "We have time. Let's use it."

I light a smoke, say, "Famous last words."

28

The Old Pinnacle Theater, otherwise known as the John Wayne Theater.

The 1920s. When the movies became a larger-than-life, steamrolling industry, they decided they needed theaters equally grand to house themselves. No mere building would suffice if it were to contain the magic of Hollywood. Becoming detailed, exotic and ornately decorated, the theaters were exciting places where stage pageants and motion pictures could be displayed the way they were meant to be seen: avant-garde.

Constructed at the height of the Roaring Twenties, the art deco styling of the Pinnacle Theater enjoyed a few years of a raucous and nearly garish existence before the Great Depression laid its withered fingers upon it. The Great Depression razed this city, leaving no stone unturned. The theater suffered just as great as its patrons and when the nation resurfaced after pummeling the Axis Powers, the theater limped along. By the start of the 1950s it eventually became known as the *Old* Pinnacle Theater.

It sat in disrepair for a while. It was a second-run theater for a while. Someone tried to make it a porno house for a while. Failed. In the '80s a new owner spent every last dime to restore the place to its original glory. He went broke doing it and sold it to a company that has since used it for marathon film festivals. Continued to this day. For weeks on end it will play

Westerns back-to-back, hence the John Wayne title. It also does marathons of Ed Wood, Universal Pictures' Classic Monsters with guys like Bela Lugosi, Boris Karloff and Lon Chaney living forever. There are some small art film shows, a festival or two.

Candy Man is four rows in front of me. *Dark glasses and he's always on the phone,* that carjacker thug said. This guy meets the description. Only an asshole wears sunglasses in a movie theater. A Blues Brother this guy ain't.

There are several patrons with us, all annoyed to varying degrees by the fact that Candy here is constantly on his phone. At the beginning of the movie he spoke quietly—though he never turned down the volume of his ringer. Now, an hour in, he laughs out loud and is profane. The ushers won't come talk to him. Maybe they have before and he showed them his iron. Maybe they have before and he clocked somebody. Maybe they can smell thug, gangbanger and drug dealer and won't chance it.

The Old Pinnacle Theater costs a whole dollar to get in. Candy hangs out near the rear entrance and exit. His customers must buy their ticket, come find him, buy their score and leave. I've seen some fellas come and do the drug deal handshake with him then sit down to enjoy the film. I've seen several turn on a heel and bolt. Why people pay to come buy drugs is beyond me. Maybe his shit is that good.

Candy gets up and walks out. I follow. I move slowly and watch him as he dials a new number on his phone, walks to the bathroom. Oh good. I bought a large soda before sitting down to start the movie. I drank half of it in a hurry to make room for whiskey. So I need to drain the lizard anyways. Two birds.

I give him some lead and then go in myself. He takes the one shitter and I take the one urinal so we wind up side by side with the thin wall of the stall between us. He's obviously put the female on speakerphone so he can wipe. But then, I hear him pop open some kind of container. I hear him tap the container and then the quiet sounds of him chopping.

Sniff.

I zip up. Think about washing my hands first but decide it'll be more fun to punch out this guy with dirty fists.

"Ronnell, you better listen to me!" The female voice, all demands and sass.

More sniffing.

"You the baby daddy of two of my kids! You ain't movin' out, you ain't fuckin' no other bitches and you ain't gonna treat me like your other baby mammas! I ain't some throw-away pussy like that! Got me, motherfucker?"

"Bitch, lower your voice," Candy man says, his voice husky. He continuously sniffs with the runny nose that coke users have.

"I ain't no bitch—"

"You a tired, play-out bitch and I got better things to occupy my time with—"

"Ronnell, I'm gonna get your momma on the phone and then we'll see who you be answerin' to. Wanna see that? Huh?"

"I said *shut up*, bitch."

Well, I've heard enough. I go to the stall door and kick it in. Candy man shoots up off the toilet, pants down around his ankles, cell phone laid across the toilet paper dispenser. His coke mirror and a small vial fall to the floor.

"What the fuck?" he shouts. His mouth is full of gold, and collapses inward as I drill him into the wall behind him.

I drag him out of the stall, all to the chorus of gleeful shouts from his phone. "Beat his cheatin' ass! Whoever you is, mother-fucker! Beat his cheatin' ass! He need to learn! But send him home now, I need my baby daddy!"

I go back into the stall, get the phone and whisper, "I'm going to kill and eat him, if for nothing else than to spare him all your bitching and moaning," and terminate the call. She immediately calls back, and I drop the phone in the toilet.

Go to work.

***

Before he comes to I dig through his pockets.

The usual: no ID, state-issued welfare debit card, two more cell phones I find just as they start to ring as well. Probably baby mamma. They go in the shitter also. Cheap gun, a wad of money which resembles a cash register since its all small denominations for making change, twelve plastic wrapped dollops of cocaine. Money in my pocket. The rest in the shitter. I must have flushed it eight times by now.

Candy Man's eyes creak open and my gun goes to his forehead.

"Where does Thuggie hang out?"

"What?"

"Thuggie. Where is he?"

"Ahh, man. I ain't no snitch—"

I slug him with the gun. The bridge of his nose opens up and spills crimson all over the tiles. I braced the bathroom door before this all began, but I need an answer quick.

"Answer me before I put you face down in the toilet and we start over."

"You think you gonna—"

Slug him again. Eyebrow splits like an over-roasted pig. He screams. I lay the gun across his throat as leverage. Press down. He wiggles and writhes, makes wet choking sounds.

"I'm waiting."

He starts to mouth something frantically. I let up on the gun. He draws a ragged breath and shouts an address. I know the place. I press down again.

"I want to make sure you're telling me the truth."

Candy Man's eyes pop out. He must have a thing against helplessly being choked to death. He tries to nod his head like a wild animal. He wouldn't be more spastic if I were electrocuting him.

"All right, I'll buy it." I let up. He gasps for air, starts to vomit. I let him roll over and he wretches across the tile. "If I get there and it's bullshit or I've been set up, I'll live. I want you to understand that. I'll live and find you. Do we have an understanding?"

He nods as he spits, dry heaves. "I ain't no snitch," he coughs out. Translation: he has more to fear from that reputation and what will happen than he has to fear from me. Fine, if he thinks that. Not true, but let him think that. It'll buy me a surprise entry into the building.

I stand. He struggles to his feet. I drill him in the back of the head and he collapses into his vomit. It's where he needs to be.

29

My phone rings as I'm washing my hands in the bathroom sink.

Knuckles are chewed up, but it comes with the gig. I look down at Candy and his shattered glasses are sitting crooked on his flat nose. At first I think it might be his cell phone since the damn thing wouldn't shut up, but it's mine. I step out of the shitter and answer it. Petticoat.

"Yeah? What's up?" I say, sticking a smoke in my lips and walking out into the sun.

"Hey, Richard. I think we should back off of the whole thing." He sounds tired. Flat. "How about I cut you a check and we call it good?"

"Why? What's changed?"

"Nothing." Nervous now. My gut starts to swim and with these few sentences I get a picture of what's going on right now. Not good.

"Petticoat, am I on speaker phone?"

"No. Why would you even ask that?"

"Shut up then and stop acting like you're setting me up. Got it?"

"Yes, but—"

"Only yes or no answers for now on. Did you email the rapist like I told you *not* to?"

Hemming and hawing. "Damn it, Petticoat, did you or did you not email the rapist?"

Like a wrecking ball of stupid: "Yes."

"Is he there with you now?"

"Yes."

"Does he have a weapon to your head?"

"Yes."

"All right. Start answering the questions with yes or no but add in details about cutting me a check. He needs to think you're working this out. Is he white?"

"Yes. I can write it now but I'll need you to hold onto to it for a week. Is that, okay?"

"Blonde hair?"

"No."

"Brown?"

"Yes. I can do that. No problem."

"Brown eyes?"

"No."

"Blue eyes?"

"Again, no. That *will* be a problem."

"Green."

"Yes. More like it. Yes."

"Tall?"

"Richard, I have to go." Those five words soaked in absolute fright. Slow time. Muffled sounds start across the phone line. Muffled struggling sounds.

"Petticoat, are you at your office?"

"Yes! Richard he's onto us! Ric—"

A wet sound comes across the line. Some gurgling. The phone drops. What I'd call the sound of writhing on carpet. I hear someone try to pick up the phone and drop it. The quiet thump of it hitting something soft. Could be the carpet again. Could be flesh.

Now I'm in the car. Speeding.

The phone picks up. Breathing. Listening. Just quiet. Listening.

"Hello, rapist," I say.

"Mmmmm...Ricky, is it? You have such deep voice," he says in a slithering tone. "Raspy."

"Thanks. I smoke. Is Petticoat dead?"

"I prefer to think of it as joining his wife."

"You just killed your cash cow."

"Cash cow? Please," he says. "It was over the moment he hired you. Blackmail works best when it is done quietly. This is easier, I think."

Three more miles.

"So, you killed Mickey Cantu as well?"

Quiet. Even his breathing stops. Then, "Who knows? Who knows..." His voice trails off like he's thinking. I can hear him cluck a time or two.

"So is that a yes?"

Instead, he says, "Do you know why I'm staying on the phone with you as you obviously race towards me, Dick?"

"Don't call me Dick, pervert. Men who can't get laid voluntarily don't get to disrespect me."

"Trying to antagonize me. Delicious."

"When did Cantu get you in on this? Why you? Are you also a burglar? Did you two work together before?"

Laughter. And that's all. Laughter.

"Pussy, when I get my hands on you—"

"So tough. So very, very tough for a man lying there, boozed unconscious as I came inside your home. You looked like such a baby, Dick. A baby who burped its milk all over itself and no one loved it enough to clean it."

"We'll work that out."

I hear a *whoosh* as the rapist's breathing gets harder. He sounds labored.

"Out of breath? Did Petticoat whip your ass before you killed him?"

"No. I'm lugging around his secretary."

I floor it. Run a red light and an old pickup truck dodges off to the side, mashing the horn as it goes.

"Let the woman go," is all I can say as I navigate the final leg with abject fury.

"Let her go? Dick, that's just plainly stupid. I've worked this hard to get her. Besides, she's already stuffed in my trunk. Do you know how much work it would be to open it, untie her, help her out and then what? Apologize? How awkward. No, no, no. She's mine."

"I will fucking kill you."

"You'll never get your hands on me, Dick."

"The crime scene. You've left DNA there."

Silence at that.

"You're not too clever when you spit on people." No comment to that one. "I've already got the sample in the lab."

A long huff. "All right, Dick. I'm going to hang up. Good luck sifting through the ashes at Petticoat's, then."

"What?"

"Ta-ta." Click. Silence.

Who ends a phone call with *ta-ta*? Really?

I turn the corner at ninety miles an hour and stop. Hit the steering wheel with a fist and hear the mounting bolts shake with the impact.

Inferno. The whole second floor of Petticoat's building, burning with a rage I feel as I realize I can do nothing. This guy has won.

30

Officers on scene. Hose draggers. The blaze was pretty good; he meant to cover his tracks well.

One charred male body inside, I told them it was probably Petticoat. The arson dick arrives and we talk. Introduced himself as Detective Greene. No idea who he is. He's efficient and brusque the way school principals from the '50s were; straight answers, no fluff, stares me down from over the rim of his eyeglasses and I think he might spank me if I zig when I should zag.

"I'll need a statement," Greene says.

"Sure."

I tell him about the DNA I have being tested, give him the old SAPD case number for the Petticoat rape. Tell him about the break-in, the print, the spit. All being tested.

"Hopefully this will ID the guy."

"Yeah."

Then of course, there's the secretary. I describe her the best I can when I saw her half-undressed and getting ready to take it, which mostly comes down to average sized boobs but they were nice. I'm sure Clevenger will put that out on an APB.

PD canvasses the area to get a description of the rapist, his car, which direction he headed in, anything. One officer comes back and said two teenage girls having a late lunch down the street saw a green car tearing ass away from here. Then the fire burst through the windows and they stopped paying attention to anything else.

Greene orders them to trace Petticoat's phone but as I'm walking around I see one smashed, lying in a puddle twenty feet from the front door of the building. I'm sure that's it. Tell the cops to ask anyone if they saw what car was parked there last. Was it green? There are two cars parked next to the space so I wait for those owners to come along so I can ask them but they never show. They might be at work. They might not want to go get their car and drive through the crowd of blue. I tell Greene and he tasks a uniform to run the plates, wait there.

I assume the secretary is already dead. I have to hope that. The rapist is taking her from crime scene number one to crime scene number two. Crime scene number two always has a body count. And since this guy has no respect for women anyways and he has already killed at crime scene number one, that girl's life, if not over already, will be miserable and agonizing until she is mercifully detached from this world. But I swear, if the rapist ruins her and then lets her live, I'll peel him apart over the course of a few weeks. I'll make him eat himself to stay alive. Hannibal Lecter will turn away from what I'll do because it will be too upsetting.

The sun begins to hide from us as the fire quiets down to embers and weak smoke. To the west, our best source of light starts to snuggle into the opposite side of the earth and damn it for doing so. Everywhere in the metro green cars being driven by a single white male are getting pulled over and rubber glove inspected. I'd love to be in on that just for the chance of pulling over the right guy. I'd never report it; I'd just release the secretary and keep the driver. Work my magic.

Finally I look at Greene and say I've got some place to be. I walk off, dial Clevenger.

He answers with, "Hey, man, that you near the arson?"

I laugh just enough to release the day's tensions. "Of course. That's my rapist's handiwork. Sewing up loose ends and cutting new ones."

"What happened?"

I tell him. When I'm done he says, "Keep your head down low, brother."

"Sure. One thing. I need a favor."

"Not a problem."

"I need you to have a records dump for Joe & Barry's Family Pawn. It's south of the river. If you can, give me a work-up on anybody who turns up connected to the place."

"You think either Joe or Barry is connected to Petticoat?"

"Don't know. That is the pawnshop Mickey Cantu would use as a fence. It's what he knew, so I imagine he went back there to get them prepped for that deal."

"I'll go with you on that one." I hear Clevenger sigh and think for a second. "You'll need this secretary. If for nothing else, she can identify your rapist. Open and shut then."

It's my turn to sigh and think for a second. "She's dead. You know that, right?"

"I don't want to know it."

"We need to find her, but she might not even be with the guy. For all we know she's in the building, still smoldering under a collapsed ceiling," I say.

"I don't know which would be worse," Clevenger says.

"I do."

Clevenger and I say our goodbyes and hang up. I get in my car. Light a smoke. Pull out and drive down the road. I need to get to this building Candy man told me about.

Half way to the building my cell rings. Unknown number.

"Hello?"

"Dick," that mix of reptilian and queer comes crawling back across the line. "Would you like to retrieve the secretary?"

"Yes." I pull over and listen intently. Any background noise on the phone, any clue or hint as to where he is. "Let her go."

"I want a hand-off. Face to face, so I may look in your eyes instead of looking down at you passed out, drunk and soaked in vomit."

"Name it. I'll be there."

"The Old Cecil's Bar. Ten minutes. No cops."

"I'll be there."

"If I even *think* a cop is around, she's dead. Her guts will spill out onto the sidewalk like I was kicking over a bucket. I will disappear forever. Do you understand my orders?" *Orderzzzzzzzzzz.*

"Of course."

"Don't be stupid, Dick. I'm better than you. You'll always do well to remember that."

"You're far more arrogant than me for sure, and I'm pretty fucking arrogant." I crush out my smoke on the dash and set my mind to doing the same to him. "Ten minutes. Is she hurt?"

Click. Silence.

I call Clevenger.

"What's up, buddy?" he says.

"Rapist called. Wants to hand-off the girl at the Old Cecil's Bar in ten minutes. Said no cops."

"Well of course, no cops. I'll call dispatch and get our ball rolling. PD will stay away then. I'd hate to not let him call the shots."

"I appreciate it. Un-marked only, and have them park a ways away. Play it so below the level James Dean would be jealous they're being so cool."

"Not a problem."

"Also, he's got something else in store. For me."

"How so?"

"He's gotten away scot-free. I've never even seen him, and now he wants a face-to-face meeting? Hand off a victim?"

"Be careful," Clevenger says. He can smell it just like I do. "Sounds like he wants to kill you."

"He's going to have to get in line," I say and pull up next to the Old Cecil's Bar. Game on.

<h1 align="center">31</h1>

The thing about Old Cecil's Bar is this: there is an *old* Old Cecil's Bar, and a *new* Old Cecil's Bar.

The original one—the *old* old one—was in a building that was trying to earn historic status. During the city inspection of it so many structural problems were exposed, the building was emptied for renovations. Not too long ago Old Cecil's Bar moved three blocks over to a better location. The original site still had Cecil's marquee up and I arrive there.

Anyway, I arrive and not more than thirty seconds later a man steps around the corner, looking respectable in decent khakis and a button-down shirt, on his arm the shivering secretary. They never look the way they sound.

"I want to commend you for the fire over at Petticoat's," I say as I walk up to him. "It shows you're not the biggest pussy in the world for only hurting women."

The rapist smiles. I absorb his every detail. Line, curve and mark. An eighth-inch scar near his mouth from where his childhood cat clawed at him? Got it. Crow's feet around his eyes means he's around forty and probably Irish? Got that, too. Nicotine stain on his front right tooth from where he smokes right-handed and mindlessly puts the cigarette on that side of his mouth.

"I'm much more than some sex-starved pervert living in his mother's basement," he says. The secretary is so wild-eyed and frazzled I'm honestly surprised she can walk. Standing next to him, she trembles and is bolt-still. "I am holding all the cards here."

"Let her go," I say, bracing. "She's just some broad who was at the wrong place at the wrong time."

"I rather enjoy her scent. I think I'll keep her here." His lower lip never moves as he speaks. His tongue curls around his every word like a sexual examination before they're allowed to leave his mouth.

"If she gets hurt, I promise I will make this last longer than your sanity can go."

"So furious over a disposable woman you don't know? I never understood the drive some men have towards protecting things that just aren't worth their own weight in dog shit."

"Try me."

He chuckles at that, like it's some inside joke. "Why do you think I asked for this meet?"

"I figured you wanted this meet to turn yourself in," I say, wondering where Clevenger's boys are.

The rapist always keeps one hand behind the secretary. I imagine he's got a heater pressed to her back. I watch that shoulder; any flicker and I draw my iron here and lay an egg in his forehead.

"I wanted to see you upright before we part ways," he says. He smirks and radiates a sense of confidence that says he's never been tested. He's just always gotten away with whatever it is he does. I would love the opportunity to shatter that like cheap ceramic. "No cops, right, Dick?"

"None." Clevenger's boys should be around here some-where. Just waiting, waiting, waiting...

"Very good," the rapist slithers. "Glad I picked Old Cecil's Bar and not the new one."

"Me too." Now I know where Clevenger's boys are. The sinking in my gut tells me so. "Funny story. I'd always get a beer here after I locked up a member of your kind."

"My kind, eh? I'm not a freak, Dick."

"Oh thank God. I'll tell Mrs. Petticoat a normal man did that to her."

"You can tell her that, if you want," he says, again with that unchallenged grin. "When you meet her in hell."

His arm still behind the secretary, that shoulder I've been watching, it moves.

I go for mine and he's faster than I'd like. He's up in my shit, an inch away from me with the secretary mashed between us. I take my hand away from my gun; hold it open so he can see. He lets a contented sound exit through his thin lips and steps back just enough to not smell my breath.

His smile is all teeth, precious and bleached white around the deep stains like he has something to prove to high society. He gives me the type of smile I'm sure he wore when he slid off Mrs. Petticoat's panties. The fulfillment. Glancing at her unconscious husband, bleeding from his forehead as he lay helpless to her.

"See the contentment in my eye?" he asks. I judge the distance between us. "I have lived a life of success. This is the natural way of things for me, Dick."

His finger is so over-wrapped around the trigger he's going to pull the shot.

"A guy like you is a cockroach, albeit a platinum one." His eyes crawl along my face like it was made of ice cream and he's a sleazy, hungry fat kid. "You sneak crumbs, disappear when shit goes down and in general are loathed by all around you."

His wrist is small. His forearm doesn't look like it could stand up in a round of golf. He's holding the gun cockeyed to begin with and when it goes off that wrist is going to fail at its one job of keeping the weapon aimed on a steady platform.

"That's where Petticoat went wrong. If he'd known you were going to sneak around his back and try and switch the black-mailing on him he would have shit a brick. He would have kept paying me. But the cockroaches like you get greedy. And fast."

The gun is a small revolver. The hammer is forward. Double-action. He's going to have to do more work to pull that trigger. He'll slap it, yank it. Maybe pull down.

"How do you feel being such a pathetic waste? I mean, I broke into your home and you were just lying there, shitting your pants. OD'ing."

"First," I say, rolling my neck loose before this happens. "I did not shit my pants. I was having a medical episode. Secondly, I wasn't backdooring Petticoat. I was trying to flush you out. And third, you know why Petticoat hired me?"

The rapist giggles. Honestly giggles. "Why, sugar?"

I hammer his gun and it clatters to the sidewalk, grab him by his throat and lift him off the ground. He eeks out a bitch scream before I squeeze too hard and it's wonderful, watching that smug fulfillment leave his face. "Because he knew I'd kill you." And I turn him upside down before I drill him into the concrete.

He buckles. Rolls with it. His scalp *smacks* off the concrete and instantly he makes a scratching play for the gun. The secretary screams. Just stands there, her mind weathered down to a few fragile nuggets, and *screams*. Grabs her hair and flexes her whole body to belt out those shrill notes.

We're not alone on this street. Other people notice. Folks begin to crowd the front window of the gym across the street. A few women with shopping bags pause down the sidewalk. Pull out a cell phone. And I'll be damned; one ballsy motherfucker comes trotting over, still in his spandex weight-lifting suit. Right over to us. The rapist, even if he is forty with crow's feet digging in around his eyes, he looks respectable in decent khakis and a button-down shirt. He's here with the secretary. So close they could have been arm-in-arm.

And then me, chewed up from fighting dudes and getting shot at all my life, a grizzly older man with a neck tattoo and a hefty five o'clock shadow. Mr. Spandex starts shouting in his best drill sergeant command voice: "Drop the gun! Cops are on their way! Stop it! ROBBERY!"

And then, since I'm still fighting the rapist to keep him from the gun when maybe I should just slug him and back up, I draw my iron, and Mr. Spandex jumps in.

To help the rapist.

Mr. Spandex gets his steroid-assisted mitts on me, tries to wrap an arm under me and around my chest in some bullshit shoulder-pin thing and I'm struggling with the rapist over a fucking gun.

"This guy is a rapist!" I shout.

"No, I'm not! Help me!" the rapist shouts back, doing his best nightingale impersonation. Mr. Spandex buys it, keeps a hold on me.

Fine. The ayes have it, then.

I gather a wad of spit and launch it right at the rapist's face. Hit him in the left eye. All gooey and yellow from a Rum Coast cigarette. He flinches, wigs out. I chop at his throat and he rolls. I shove the gun off and away from us, turn to Mr. Spandex. He's gritting his teeth and trying to squeeze me like we were competing in some homoerotic underground fighting ring. I throw an elbow like I'm trying to drive a nail into brick and get enough of his nose to work some magic. He jumps to his feet, runs across the street and nearly gets creamed by some teenage broad worried about texting as opposed to driving.

I spin around. The rapist has the gun. Aims it. The sun glints off it now for the second time.

The secretary just keeps screaming, today's events no doubt charging several years in the future to her psychologist's bill. I drill a right cross and land it on the rapist's cheek and for the first time in a long time I see the eyes of a man who thought one thing but learned another.

He thought he was running this show and I just put a crimp in it. Big time.

The rapist shoves the secretary towards me and fires a round. I'm not hit and maybe she is, maybe she's not. Mr. Spandex is across the street crying like a bitch, coddling his nose. Done with the one fight he'll be in for his entire life. The secretary's heel snaps off and I don't look back. She collapses, might be dead. But she's free of the man I'm trying to beat to a pulp and I start doing the one thing in police work I truly hate: foot chase.

Charging towards the shoreline, crowds get in the way.

Not five hundred feet from where we started, and my sixty-year-old smoker's lungs are about done with this. The rapist isn't a runner, but he is a survivor. I'm not a runner, but I am a hunter.

We hit people. Thick crowd. Some kind of sidewalk art fair. He tumbles through; I plow. The smell of human cattle hits my nostrils, all sweat and nervous energy. Elbows and shoulders get in the way, like I need a machete to cut through the overgrowth. Start pushing, needing deep but unsatisfying breaths for my burning lungs.

The rapist shoots glances back at me every few seconds because he knows what's going to happen when I get my hands on him. I knock over a display and a canvas clatters off into the street. "Hey!" Some dweeb in a beret and a plaid shirt buttoned up to his Adam's apple shouts and jumps off a high-legged chair. "My *art!*"

The rapist comes to a grinding halt in the middle of the crowd. Spins to face me. We make eye contact and I smile. Taste the blood in the water. Then he juts his arm in the air, ready to make these human cattle stampede.

His gun fires a shot off to the heavens, and the crowd goes batshit crazy like ants after a kid stomps their mound.

Screams, scattering, panicked chaos.

He sets off at a dead sprint and I give what I have to follow. Art fair folks dodge into shop fronts and behind cars. Strollers with sleeping babies zoom past with harried moms shoving them along.

The rapist grabs an old woman and throws her to the ground. If he's trying to put something in my path his aim is way off. But then he grabs another woman and throws her. Then a young man. Adds in a trashcan for color, then another man.

I kick the trashcan and jump over one of the dudes. The rapist runs around a corner. I take it wide in case he's going to jump me. Nope. It leads down a short alleyway, and there he is, knocking over more debris. A stack of empty cardboard boxes, more trash cans. He clears the other end and I bull rush through the obstacles.

He wanted the meet so he could taunt and then shoot me. He never dreamed of this. It says something about a man who runs and hurts people along the way rather than go toe-to-toe. You've got to be careful with that type. Cowards, but when things don't go their way they take cheap shots.

I see him go over a hill with the bay behind him. He's making for a brand new subdivision. It's all vertical townhouses done in tight rows. Adorned with banners, balloons galore and a big sign which reads: TODAY! OPEN HOUSE!

He darts in the first house, the one with the open and inviting front door.

I hear gasps and shouts as I enter. There is a guided tour going on with a real estate agent in the front. The rapist shoves through a group of them and shoots a glance over his shoulder. I'm in; our eyes meet. He takes off. ALL BAMBOO FLOORS! rushes past me in a blur set to concerned shouts. ENERGY EFFICENT! TRIPLE-PANED WINDOWS! SAFE NEIGH-BORHOOD! TWO BLOCKS FROM THE BEACH!

Up the stairs, knocking over an easel with some pie chart display on it. I get to the top and the people there are cautious, nervous, stealing glances, no doubt in disbelief over this. Us, bursting through their wet dream of a new luxury home. Soiled it with the gleaned knowledge that once I get my hands on him I'm going to beat him to death.

Hallway runs both ways. Window in front of me, rooms on both sides. Second flight of stairs beside me, running to floor number three. These homes are too narrow to have much square footage on a single level. They're stacked. Hipster-style. My lungs want an elevator.

Where to? Not up. I would have heard it. Hold my breath. Tune out my heart. The gaggle of people down below has raised their nervous chatter to a cacophony. I need the rapist to give me a sound. I dart to the left, throw open a door. Clear the room in three seconds and out. Next door. Nothing. That's it for this end. Past the stairs, next door is the shitter, spacious, marbled, gaudy gold trim and fixtures. Lifted right out of Saddam Hussein's palace.

Maybe he waited until I ducked in a room, ran past me down the hall. I jump into the hallway, listen for feet up the stairs. Can't tell. At the stairs I look up. Hear down below, "*I can't believe this! The nerve—*" "*way to screw up the day—*" "*probably a drug quarrel or they're boyfriends and one of 'em—*" "*I called the fucking the cops, they never show up when—*" "*if these are the neighbors—*"

"Shut the fuck up!" I bellow, rattle windows.

Gasps down below. Sweet silence; the living room is now a bone yard. Then—

Up the stairs. A sudden crash. I might be old, but I know the sound of a hip hitting furniture. He's on the third floor. Two at a time then, the all bamboo flooring passes under my determined feet.

Third floor, movement to the right. I take cover behind some obnoxious balustrade that extends halfway to the ceiling and probably needs its own support beam. I check around it and aim my heater. Nothing. Nothing—

Sounds from outside. Up here? Not floating up from below. The AC is on; vent is right next to me, coughing ice up my pant leg. Down the hall, a real estate banner flutters. Breeze.

Open window.

Escape.

I go, muzzle leading the way. Too fast to give him any reaction time. Swoop into a bedroom. The room itself takes a sharp gasp I run in it so determined. Picture window, open. His feet on the sill, his ass ducking under the limits of the sliding glass. Hands outside, grabbing the house's frame. He turns his head just enough to see me and pushes off.

Third story window, gone.

I get to it, see how the roof slopes out under the window to brace the rapist's fall.

He's sliding down into a corner made by two peaks, looks back and smirks. I aim my gun just as he goes over. I holster and shove through the window. Move fast enough along the slope to lose my footing. Fall on my side, skid down too fast. Scramble. Kick a foot up into this corner and kick the other foot up into that, claw the shingles. I stop, crabwalk down. Get to the corner and peer over, see the rapist.

He's clubbing a man over the head, carjacking his truck. I can see the brake lights on, idling in the driveway of the open house. The rapist jumps in, and I leap off the roof.

I'm floating above the truck bed as the truck roars to life, taking my flatbed landing site with it.

I catch the tailgate of the truck across my gut and I just know I'm going to shit blood over this.

The rapist is mashing the gas pedal and the truck rockets off, fishtailing out onto the road. He heads east. I give the best heave I've got and flop into the bed, roll over. Draw my iron. I go to get my balance and the rapist is watching me in the rearview mirror, hands clamped on the steering wheel like he's dangling from a cliff with only that wheel to keep him safe.

Sees the gun. Yanks the wheel. I hit against a sidewall, fight to not get thrown out. Gun moves. Yanks again. I drop to my knees, one hand holding the bed, the other swings up to the back of the truck bench.

He drives the vehicle right up and over a curb and right under the low hanging branch of a mighty oak. The force of the branch scraping along the truck's roof squeals with angry metal losing its paint job. Branches to my face, the vivid scent of fresh leaves being torn. I duck; thrust the gun forward and just squeeze off a round.

The truck yanks again, hard. I roll, hit the sidewall. Gun comes out of my hand. I scramble for it, but those floating eyes in the rearview mirror see me. Slam on the breaks. I thrust forward, make eye contact.

I'll regret it later but I punch through the sliding glass window, reach for him. He guns the engine. I grab a fistful of hair before I fall back. The hair gives before his skull does.

I rock back; hit my head on my own gun. Cut. Bleeding some. Shake the clinging hair from my fingers, grab the weapon. See those eyes. See ahead of us, how those eyes are so fixated on me they don't see where the road up ahead makes a ninety-degree turn. He jumps the curb where the road doesn't go, hits sand.

Those townhomes were two blocks from the beach. Hard to believe we're only two blocks away from where this started.

The truck yaws, goes up on two wheels. I know what's coming; don't want any part of it. The sand has gnawed at the speed, and I dive like an Olympic swimmer right off the ass end of this thing. Hit hard. No breath. Roll with it, roll with it. Settle out.

Sand in my eyes, my nose, my mouth. Cough, look up. Truck flops sideways and stops sliding on the beach. The high tide reaches out and licks me wet. My gun ten feet in front of me. I try to get to my feet and it hurts. I go anyways. Feel the constrictor around my chest, not letting me breathe. I do it slowly, shoot a glance at my right fist as I make it over to the truck. Red. Punching the back windshield opened me up. Maybe broke my middle finger. I come around the truck.

Empty.

Footprints in the sand. Small but steady trickle of hot red around them. Across the street, I see his shirt disappear under an overpass.

Right into traffic.

Four busy lanes already zigzagged and jack knifed. Honking. Hear someone's grill smash someone's bumper. Across from me, the rapist. Back turned, running towards a gym. I check to make sure I'm not going to get blitzed by a soccer mom hurrying to the next karate lesson. I go through the traffic mess as fleet-footed as a laboring man like me can.

The rapist goes into the gym. I'm about fifty feet behind.

The blast of air conditioning hits; startles my skin into shock.

The front desk is staring. Some blonde gal, big tits and tight shirt, some dude, his pretty muscles spilling out of his polo. Perfect hair all around.

"Where did he go?"

The blonde stares absently like I just asked her what two plus two equals. The dude's brain puzzles out what I am talking about, says, "The other guy?"

"No, you fucking meathead, Amelia Earhart," I say, looking both directions. "Yes! The other sweaty, beat-up dude who busted through these doors ten seconds ago!"

The blonde points to my left. I go. Over my shoulder I say, "Call the cops. Say the guy from the murder/arson is here!"

I go past a wall of windows. Weights, cardio. A pool to my left. An aerobics studio where, by all appearances, a female instructor has just finished a class. She has a sheen of sweat, fiddling with the sound system.

A startled shout from up ahead. I go. Two other aerobics women look shocked. Mumbles, "What an asshole—" and then I show up.

"Where's the asshole?"

The mumbler motions to the door beside her. Labeled WOMENS LOCKER ROOM. I hear one more muffled shout inside. I nod. "Makes sense, I guess."

Look at the women; see how their eyes light up with that *oh shit* face when my iron appears from my suit coat. I'm sure this is the most real thing which has ever happened in their tennis club lives. "Go to the front. Cops are coming. Direct them back here."

Push open the door, gun drawn.

Eight stalls with their doors shut and a massive running shower room.

This is a *Revenge of the Nerds* wet dream. The locker room door opens to a small anteroom, and that opens to the rows of shitters and four sinks. That opens to the showers. I imagine beyond them are lockers.

But all eight stall doors shut? And I smell something. Not sweat, not chlorine. Not the musty humidity of running hot water. Grime. Gutter hooch and grime.

Duck down, look for feet. One set of obvious woman's feet and the far end, left side. Labored heart beat thudding in my temples. Try to control my ragged breathing. Burned the inside of my throat. Sandpaper inhales, acid exhales. Sweat has had time to react to the sixty-eight-degree temperature inside here. Clothes wet, torn. Can feel the way my socks are soaked and bunched between my toes. Eyes sting with runoff from my forehead. This isn't how I want to clear a room.

In through the nose, feel the weight of the air as it settles at the very bottom of my lungs. Burns. Out through my pursed lips, cracked and tired from snarling.

He is in here. In one of these shitters. The athletic, nude women in the shower room wouldn't be still scrubbing their exhausted, tight little bodies if that skeezy pervert ran through. It figures that I get this fantasy in real life and there's someone I have to kill to distract me from it.

Gun aimed midpoint on the first door on the left, I try it. Swings in, nothing. The one on the right, empty. Next one on the left, empty. Next one on the right? Locked. There were no feet below the door when I checked.

Giddy as a schoolgirl. Trigger finger excited, mind's eye

squeezed down to a tight reticle, air going in and out in harmony with the river of death I wade out into, thoughts clear now. This is it.

My back pressed to the stall behind me, I knock on the locked one. No answer. *"Hello? Hola? Housekeeping. Servicio de limpieza."* Nothing. "Any rapists hiding in there?"

No answer.

"Okay. I'll try the next one—" And he bursts out of the one where the woman's feet were, his gun firing. I dart down, draw a bead. No go. Locked stall, a decoy. I dive into the next one up. Drop for a split second. See his feet scramble. No plan beyond jumping out and shooting. No doubt, he's all out of lead now. I come out, bull rush. The stall with the woman's feet whisks by in an instant, an unconscious woman plopped down on the stool with her eyes closed, head against the wall. He tries to run.

"You zigged when you should have zagged, motherfucker." And in an instant, I have my mitts on him. Awesome.

We go down in a crumple. I drop a haymaker and lay open his nose in one gush of crimson. He scrambles like a turtle on its back with one miracle foothold. Shoves out, clawing for purchase on the tile. I lunge, get him. Slide just enough to feel wet. Shower room. Athletic, nude women, scrubbing their exhausted, tight little bodies until that shot rang out. He and I land at their feet. Their wet and naked feet.

Double awesome.

"Don't mind us, ladies," I say, smirking as I grab his throat. "Please, keep cleaning yourselves."

They scream, cram into one creamy bunch in a corner. Rapist is bleeding everywhere, gouging at my face. I draw back, slug him again. His jaw pops under my fist and his eyes turn bright red. He kicks, grazes my balls. Goes for my gun in the holster. One hand to guard it. I twist. He twists opposite; gets both legs free. I take the finger on my gun, yank hard enough to feel it give under my tension. He screams. Kicks again. My hand chops at his throat. Not a good one. Thumb to his eye. A little better. We're getting fucking soaked. He spasms, kicks and wiggles. Gets my knee. I slip off. His hand comes free, tries to bolt for it. I grab an ankle, yank. He tumbles forward, hits the showerhead tower. Knocks a bunch of soap and shampoo to the floor. Whishing around in the water, I pull on his ankle, get to my knees. Throw a punch. Lands poorly. He rakes at my face with a safety razor. I get a glimpse of a bunch of armpit whiskers stuck between the blades at it comes by my face. I thrust up at his jaw with my palm. The thing is already swollen twice its size and my strike makes him yelp like a puppy getting neutered awake.

I grab the first shower bottle at my feet. See something about *pumice rub* and *exfoliating* and figure it has little grains of something in it. Great.

I squeeze the bottle and a jet of it sprays across the room like this were the world's most ludicrous money shot. Hits him right in the face. But more importantly, his eyes. He grabs at them.

I stand up, trying to look as cool as I can with all the naked women. Of course, they've all beat feet. I would have thought they'd stick around to watch an uber-male like myself decimate a sex predator, but oh well. The cop in me says cuff him—not that I carry handcuffs anymore—and wait for back up. PD must be through the front door now.

The rapist writhes; splashing shower water in his face before he blinks too much and the scrubby-grains rub through his eyeballs. Get to his brain. Exfoliate that. I decide one more punch for the road should do it.

Grab him by the collar. Up on his feet. Defeated. "An ugly end to such a cocky piece of shit like you," I say. He's got nothing. He's a million miles away down a hole from where we met on the street, him so confident that the situation was his to toy with. Funny how folks like the rapist—those who have never been tested; given a false sense of security—have their worlds shattered with one good punch. Conquered. Even his hands fall away, complete in their domination. Rear back, wind up.

And then the smear floods down. I think it's shower water and try to mentally brush it away. But it's not going anywhere. Big Fry smear. A single trickle cascades, drawing behind it a million more like a freight train. A horse-drawn stampede on the backs of bulls done up in a psychedelic rainbow. Brain-frying. Gut-wrenching. I taste bile as the edges of my vision tingle with that certain special *fuck you* I get every time my noggin goes rogue. My mind numb. Muscles jelly. A swirl of mixing pastels before me, splashing my world and all it ever knew with a food fight of color. I try to swing. Just knock him out and we can be buddies lying here on the floor. No swing will come. I want it want it need it demand it but nothing.

I barely feel it as I hit the floor, shower water draining into my open, twitching mouth. The colors go dark. My brain goes dark. I go dark.

When I come to, I hear cops shouting back near the stalls. The rapist, he's long gone.

32

Spent four hours with Saint Ansgar's finest.

One in handcuffs until Clevenger showed up and argued that *I* was not the rapist. His blood washed down the drain. His trail of destruction was hastily tied together. They missed some parts but they'll connect the dots eventually. Written statement. Interviewed on a dash cam in the back of a squad car.

The chief is through the fucking roof. Shots fired, car wrecks, chases. The chief himself comes up to the scene. Sees me. Storms up.

"Well fuck me at a brisk trot, Richard Dean Fucking Buckner," he says. The chief spent four years as an Army drill sergeant and it shows. Gets up in my face, trying to lean in the way they do with recruits. Command hand, the whole nine yards. "How is it a guy like you isn't even a cop anymore and you're still here at *my* crime scene with your dick imprint everywhere I look?"

"Because I was working this case—"

"You weren't working shit!" His command hand goes right up to my head and I'm two seconds away from breaking those fingers. He can plume his feathers all he wants; his actual bite is dull. I *know* I still have teeth. "You were working on destroying *my* city! Anything else you accomplished was ancillary!"

"Out of every cop standing here, only one of 'em had this guy in his possession."

The chief coughs a mocking laugh. "All right, Dirty Harry, where is the motherfucker then?" He holds up his hands and tours the area, looking lost and confused. "Please, display your great catch. Turn him over to me and I'll give you the best citizen's arrest award I can get past the city council."

Clevenger shakes his head. "He had the rapist, Chief. But that God-awful Big Fry overdose rose up—"

"I ain't fuckin' talkin' to you, Detective!" the chief shouts.

"What he said was I had him. But you remember that huge Big Fry bust I got all those years ago that helped lock up three guys you could never nail when you were the Narcotics Commander? Remember that? That shit crept up while I was putting the gotchas on him. And while I was seizing on the ground he ran off. And none of your boys on the outside—"

"Shut up, Buckner." The chief has ice on those words. Quiet; an arctic fury. He gets close, and still thinks that because I call him Chief I'll give him the leeway of one. "You got jumped by some two-bit thugs because you never could watch your back. Any crook on the streets knew if they wanted to stand a chance against a brute Jarhead ape like you, all they had to do was stay out of your wingspan. You got OD'd by your own faults. *I* had those shitbags. Fuck you if you think you and Garrett did anything besides cherry pick my work."

Close now, nose-to-nose. "I tell you what, Richard. Be the best witness you can be for the real cops, and then stay close to home. The DA might just want to talk to you."

"If it bothers you that I'm the best cop out there for your people to learn from, so be it," I say, finger in his chest. "You can hen peck me all you want to, but never forget that every time you've been close to something, *I've* already gotten there."

"Except the rank of Chief."

"Only because I wanted the streets, not a desk and all the city council dick-sucking I could stomach."

"Look what it got you—" he says. I walk off. He takes a few steps after me, but even he knows better. Walking away I can see his shadow cast long and beside me, jumping up and down, waving his arms. Bits of words float to me from his vitriolic rant. Words like alcoholic. Brutal. Has-been and probably-a-murderer.

I don't listen. I need a drink before I find the rapist and kill him.

Clevenger calls.

The secretary is no help. Shell shock; spent most of her time in the rapist's trunk. Can't ID the make or model. Parked somewhere near the meet at the bar. Cops have canvassed the area, running every tag. He's long gone.

Tells me Willibald's funeral is early next week. Wants me to come. I agree, get off the phone. Taped my right middle finger to my right ring finger. Might not be broke, but I could have used some stitches. Never got them. Get lost in the ice cubes of a scotch; the way all the angles turn smooth and roll along one another. How they refract the light through the booze. Leathery browns, sweet caramels. They all taste like oblivion.

Beyond it, the front door to my apartment. Braced tight with a chair under the doorknob. No break-ins. Bleary and stupored, I sink into my couch.

Then I sink further, and wash away from this life for a while.

33

Late evening

Back in the day this was some Protestant office building.

Built in the '90s next door to a church which has now changed hands a number of times, sits the square, no-curb-appeal block of dilapidated shit where Thuggie supposedly hangs out. It's in the right neighborhood. Has the right graffiti sprayed along the walls. The right ghetto sleds parked beside it.

Late night. Stillness abounds the way it does when the darkness is lazy; ebon layers tossed like gauze sheets across the world. When I move a step, adjust on the concrete, I can hear the pebbles beneath my shoes collide like landsliding boulders. That loud in this stillness.

Only three windows alight. Top floor. No silhouettes. No noises. Front door; dumb idea. Back door; just as stupid. Fire escape; why not?

There's only so much *quiet* a lumbering man like me can maintain when he is precariously balanced on an alleyway trashcan as he reaches for a secured fire escape hatch.

I do it the best I can. Grab the frame, heave up. Stalk through the darkness, up the steps. Shadow passing by shadow, trying to avoid the metal creaks and groans like dead givea-ways.

Third floor, two darkened windows down from the lit ones. I get to the glass and realize I didn't really come with a plan beyond entering the building and hurting people. I brought enough lead. My travel-sized lock picking kit. A glasscutter. And, of course, my dancing shoes.

Inside, murmuring quiet. Just nothing. I squat down; cut the glass by the window lock's latch. Tap in it; listen for alerts as the fragment falls noiselessly. Undo the latch, throw the window. *Lucy, I'm home.* The annoying wash of a lingering stench of weed. Mixes with cheap liquor. The carpet is pock-marked with cigarette burns. Stains. The walls have all been painted by graffiti artists.

No sounds. Corner room. The two darkened windows I was outside of lead into here. Dead space. There are two doors leading out; one to the lighted room and one to somewhere beyond. Something tingles my guts. Crawls along my skin like an insect. Set up.

I go to the dark door, stand near it for some time. Minutes drizzle along. There is a smattering of shitty furniture here. I take a cue from my own place and get a chair. Brace the door. Now, if fools are lying in wait on the other side, I'll get a head's up before they storm in.

But something tells me my efforts are lost.

I go to the lit door. A halo of light outlines the thing; a square phantasm in this graveyard corner room. I take the handle. Turn. Shove. Duck to the side; wait for the barrage of hot lead.

Nothing.

They're better than that. Okay. Take hold of a small chair beside me. Throw it in. Clatters, bangs around. Falls and settles.

Still nothing.

I play a hunch. Step inside the doorway.

Conference room made up like it was a thug's cathedral.

Graffiti murals tell the exploits of this rabble. Stations of the Thuggie. The door I step through leads into the empty space, twenty feet long and twelve feet wide. A door directly across from me all the way down, leads to the hallway and far, far away. Two windows to my right. Light left on. A small table in the center of the room. Bears a message for me.

The first mural starts to my left. They work down the wall towards the opposite wall, follow it to the right and come back up towards me. That first mural is a colorful piece showing the art's central figure—I gather from the labels painted at his feet this is actually Thuggie—as he stands before a man on his knees. In Thuggie's right hand is the man's bleeding heart, torn from his chest. Must be a vivid and bullshit depiction of the guy he killed that Andre from the 39th Street Felons told me about.

The next shows Thuggie head and shoulders above a crowd of young men. His arms outstretched like he were a savior welcoming his flock. The neighborhood behind him cracked and disheveled. The third shows Thuggie sitting at a desk, piled high with money. Guns. Weed and white powder. Symbols of his greatness.

They go on all around the room. Artwork displaying Thuggie as half Messiah and half Scarface.

I walk over to the table. Six bottles of cheap swill rest on it. A note, poorly scribed in pen by someone who is functionally illiterate.

We commin for U
Have a dirnk on me
Kil the lites when U leive BITCH
THUGGIE

So, Candy Man squealed. I'll go back and look for him but he's gone. No doubt about it. This note says a few things. One, they don't know who I am. They're just trying to scare me off. They know what I can do, not the least of that is breaking their people. Making them talk. Two, they're afraid of me. They knew I was going to show, and rather than face me, they scatter and leave a note. Pussies.

This isn't even my brand. Turn off the lights when I leave.

Please.

All six bottles get emptied along the floor and walls. I turn off the lights as I step out; touch my lighter to the alcohol trail I left into the hallway. A blue flame sparks to life; runs away from me down the hall like it owes me money. Into the cathedral.

Booze flames shoot up the walls like a reverse waterfall. Oranges and yellows snapping all around like they were little cavorting devils and I, Satan himself, just told them to make tonight count. The heat swims around, comes at me in waves. I start to hear little pops and cracks. Things are picking up.

Black boils where the reds once were. A cancer of infernos devouring the construction. I back up, making sure the paints on the walls blister and curl before I leave. Thuggie's murals reduced to simmering splotches of running paint. Good enough. Just as the first panels of the suspended ceiling cave in, I turn around.

I go out the front door. Flames snapping and raging in the windows above me.

I turned out the lights all right, motherfuckers.

34
Saturday morning

"I'm looking for Joe Clarke," I say, hating the smell of inside an old folks' home.

Prunes and convalescents wheel about. Some skit-skat along, others hobble, one woman sits in her wheelchair, staring off into whatever great void she's trying to go down, one hand listlessly fiddling with her catheter's collection bag.

The double front doors behind me, sunlight pouring in like a great temptation to make a run for it. The front desk before me, one overweight caretaker plopped into her seat, her carrot-red hair dye job glowing about her scalp. Rather than get up to look for the man, she turns in her chair; a tremendous heave and shifting of all her rolls and bulges. Too much make-up, too little of anything else.

A stubby finger jabs at a man. "That's old Joe," she says. "You family?" she asks, out of breath from exerting herself by turning in a chair.

"I knew him from his days at the pawn shop," I say. Step away.

"I didn't know he worked at a pawn shop," said with a fake chipper reserved for customer service jobs.

"Don't care if you did," I mumble, walk towards him. Joe Clarke is sitting on a bench, clearly visible through a glass side door. The door opens to a large, meandering court yard. Maybe it will smell better than the mélange of stale urine, antiseptic and unwashed-and-nearly-dead people in here.

Outside, I sit down on the bench. Joe looks over.

"I know you?"

"My name's Richard. As long as I've worked in the city I must have driven by your shop a thousand times. Always saw your name next to Barry's on that big yellow sign."

"Yeah, but do I *know* you?"

"I guess not, but I thought I'd come by—"

"Whatever bullshit you're sellin', I'm not here to listen." Joe turns away, crosses his arms.

"You ran a blue-collar criminal enterprise fencing stolen goods through your pawn shop."

He gets hard. Looks back at me, the lines in his face set. "Don't know you. Fuck off."

"Mickey Cantu's last gig was going down after he got out of prison. I say last gig because he involved someone from *your* pawnshop and that someone betrayed and murdered him, then raped a woman. She's dead also." I stare at him.

"I know no such thing." He rocks forward and tries to stand but his back and knees aren't in the mood. He rocks back, settles on the bench. Gears up for another try and I put a hand out. He stays seated.

"All I want is a name."

"You think you can show up to a halfway decent raisin ranch like this one and point at some old man and then accuse him of bein' around rapists and murderers? What, did you pawn me your wife's weddin' ring and I sold it before you could buy it back? Is that it?"

"*All I want is a name.*"

"I got news for you, jack. If you don't want me sellin' your shit, don't give me the chance."

I lean in, one hand on his shoulder. "Listen, if I wanted to shake you down, I'd wait until you were in your room and struggling to take a piss and then do it. But I respect your dignity. I will *not* respect your bullshit. I used to be on the force, and I know dozens of guys like you. Stan Carlson from over on 82nd and Perry. Tom just off of interstate by the stadium. Enrique Mendez always had that asshole rooster running around inside his shop. When Bill Mahoney was robbed and murdered, I worked the case and got the bad guy. *I* did that.

"I'm sure when you opened you were legit, but as the neighborhood went downhill you had to fence to make the rent. Mickey Cantu was a good guy who liked being a cat burglar. The problem is, he walked into a set up and got axed for it. And he was set up by your employee. Now give me the name."

Joe stares off. No doubt he knew Stan and Tom and Enrique and Bill. No doubt he, like everyone who ever met Bill, hated Bill. It was only a matter of time that guy got shotgunned to death standing at his cash register, but it doesn't make it right. I let it all sink in. Lean away. Sit down next to him.

"I never knew no Mickey Cantu," he says. "But if you got reason to believe it was my shop..."

I pull out my Rum Coasts, offer him one. Joe looks over my shoulder at the desk, shrugs. Takes one. I light us both. Then I say, "Mickey made a deal with some guy he met in prison. Rob the house while the guy is out with his wife, Mickey keeps the score; the guy gets to claim his insurance. Only Mickey got a second dude in on it and that dude killed him and waited at the house. Raped—"

"Ursa Hanchett," Joe says without even looking at me. "Couldn't have been anyone else in my crew. *If* it was one of my employees, it was Ursa Hanchett."

Sounds like a pervert.

I nod, sit back. Joe takes a drag, scratches his chest. Says, "Hanchett's old man, Bob, he waddn't half-bad. He had a temper, but that man could eyeball somethin' and nail the worth. Never was off, neither. Like those goofs on that travelin' antiquities show where you bring your junk and they tell you the history and all that? That was Bob. And he loved that boy. But that boy was like...a snake or somethin'. Even when he was a kid I says—I says to my wife, 'Francine, that Hanchett boy is either a fruit or a serial killer. He's too soft and too connivin'.' That's what I says."

"And you think he was the rapist?"

"He had some mental thing. Back in the day if they wasn't right we'd just whisper, say they was retarded or whatever, but the kid could do math just fine and he, you know, he wasn't like he was gonna need to live with his dad his whole life. But he was...*off.* There'd be months and months where the kid was nice and sweet and very likeable, he'd come around with girls and all that. Pretty girls, too. Some were from the right side of the tracks, others weren't, but he was one of those guys that if he set his sights, he had 'em. But then he had this cruel streak.

"Probably 'cuz his mom...Bob picked all the lookers but not a one of 'em had any substance to her. Not a damn one. Ursa's mom was gorgeous when she wasn't drunk and trying to cut Bob with his shaving razor. Crazy bitch. Messed that boy up for life when she killed herself on the boy's birthday. Yeah. Crazy bitch did it on purpose, I just know it. Bob always ran Ursa around like he was his pet or somethin', for sure. He loved that boy, but he was weird about him, too. The whole thing was weird. But I blame the mom."

Joe smokes for a minute. "Ursa'd steal from me, I know that. Just sneaky enough to be a pain in the ass. He waddn't so good he'd be a world-class criminal; he was just such an annoyance that the only reason why I never beat his ass once real good was Bob. I could never take Bob. And I needed Bob. So I put up with his perv boy."

"Sounds like a deviant in the making," I say, putting together the profile in my head.

"Yeah. Like I says, he was two-faced. Either he was the best guy ever, or he was a damned animal. And a cruel one. I had this niece from my older brother's side. Her name was Cassy and she wound up posin' nude in some skin magazine. Ursa knew I wasn't proud of it so he went and got that magazine, tore out her pictures. Then the bastard would leave them a few at a time around the shop for all my customers to see. Little stuff like that. Little stuff. That's all."

But that's how it starts. When God makes a new baby, they're a clean slate. Ready to be directed. Molded. And then unstable women get pregnant by morally ambiguous men, and you get a little boy who loves his mother for what he wants her to be, hates her for what she is, gets a power-complex from his controlling father and eventually sees his mother in every woman he meets. Ta-da.

"Did he have any siblings? What happened to Bob?"

"Ah, hell. Bob was with another woman a few weeks after Ursa's mom died. I think he married her. She had kids, he had a kid. They had some kids together. Two mutts tryin' to be the *Brady Bunch* if you ask me. Bob's dead now. Heart attack or a stroke. Somethin'. His wife's dead, too. I never kept a bead on the kids. Hell, I don't even think Bob called the boy Ursa. He called him somethin' else entirely. The world knew the kid as Ursa, though. Look for Ursa Hanchett. As far as where he is now, I dunno. I quit carin' 'bout Bob when he quit workin' for me, if I'm bein' honest."

"Joe, thank you. I appreciate your help. Ursa has killed another man. The husband of the woman he raped."

"This Mickey fella?"

"I think he killed Mickey, yes. But the guy Mickey met in prison and made the deal with, I *know* Ursa killed that guy."

"Oh. I see it now. Well, go get 'em. Set fire to 'em."

"I'm going to try," I say.

The courtyard door opens and Chunk from behind the desk is standing there, hands on her hips. Looking like a penguin. "No smoking, Joe and Joe's friend. Joe, you figure you know better with your ailment."

"My cancer's goin' kill me whether I smoke or not," Joe

grumbles, flicks his butt out into the grass. "So suck it."

Penguin huffs and turns around. I stand.

"Thank you for the help." I drop the rest of my pack and the lighter on the bench next to him.

Joe looks up. "I just bought TVs, jewelry and guitars. Somebody had somethin' to sell, and I bought it. That's all."

"I know." He never looked for the blood, so it must not have ever been there to begin with.

We shake hands and I leave. Call 4-1-1, ask for the Yellow Pages. Ask for an address for a Mister Ursa Hanchett. Get it; he's the only one in the book. Go there.

Help myself inside.

35

I have been inside the lairs of monsters before and they're never quite what you'd expect.

In 1988 I worked on the Metro Squad to round up Dennis Mangeala, a serial killer with four corpses to his name. He lived in his mom's basement, toys from the 1970s and onward still in their packages, dusted and neatly arranged on display. Interspersed between original *Star Wars* figures, *GI Joes*, *Transformers* and cereal box collectibles were bones from the elderly women he attacked and dismantled. Torture-erotica magazines were filed with his comic books. Superman and Wolverine adorning covers neatly cataloged alongside others featuring a man taking a blow torch to his crank, and other such scenes.

Jorge Ramirez-Sanchez, back in 1990, I think. Used a cordless drill on his wife and mother-in-law. Mailed pictures of them to family and his church. His place was a quaint bungalow, lots of sunlight filtering in through the blinds. Plush carpet. Empty refrigerator with the exception of a carton of strawberry yogurt.

Camille Dobey, her studio apartment divided in half. She painted the north side entirely black and filled the walls with heavy metal posters and all poser-Goth, vampires and werewolves shit. The south half was drenched in white with every imaginable religious symbol from around the world. Yin and yang, I guess. She would walk by people in the streets, slashing with razors she'd dip in Drano. We had her surrounded on 4th

185

and 10th Avenue when she slit her own throat. Most women go for something cleaner, but not her. Blood everywhere.

Ursa Hanchett. The air in the place is oily and cool as it slithers along my skin. No sound. A faint bleach smell teases the air. Carpet, a living room that flows into a dining room and kitchen. I see two doors, no doubt one a bedroom and one a bath. The doors are opposite each other, both slightly ajar. I walk up and open the left door first. Bedroom. No Ursa. Bath. No Ursa.

He has an old black and white photo on his kitchen counter, turned to face the living room. It's a woman. I'm guessing his mother. Her clothes smack of the late sixties or early seventies. Same with the hair. Good looking, but even in the picture I can see what Joe was talking about. *Gorgeous when she wasn't drunk and trying to cut Bob with his shaving razor. Crazy bitch.* She just has an aura.

And what's even more unsettling is how much she looks like Carla Gabler. If Mickey had gotten her involved in Petticoat's burglary I bet there would have been two rape victims that night.

The sink in the bathroom has blood droplets on it. Used cotton balls stained a reddish brown. Peel-apart bandage wrappers scatter on the floor like errant snowflakes from a light dusting. Tweezers. Hair clippers still plugged into the wall and patches of shaved hair settled everywhere. A bloody thumbprint on the mirror.

Good. I fucked this guy up.

I open his linen closet, which apparently doubles as a medicine cabinet. He's got prescription bottles lined up along one shelf. All opiates. They all have names on them, but none of them are his. Stolen, then, or bought off the street. Junkie. I count eight bags of cotton balls, plus the one in the bathroom he used on his wounds.

For such a small space, Ursa has lots of very expensive electronics. Top notch everything. HDTV, bluetooth-connected surround sound system. An awe-inspiring computer system. Wireless everything. Little gadgets galore. Video cameras, tablets, remotes to things I don't even know where they are.

If I had all the time in the world I'd have Clevenger run the serial numbers through NCIC. I imagine most of this stuff is hot. But I don't have the time.

Bedroom closet, then. He has so little space to hide things here; this is the obvious choice. And, bingo.

Immediately I start to flash to my closet where I keep my wife's things.

The strange hot and cold of basking in the aura of my wife's radiance, snap out of it and be here, in this reptile's hidey-hole. In my mind's eye my wife's pictures are along the left-hand wall. Ursa has women's panties nailed to it. Nine pairs.

"Did he take a trophy from your wife? A memento of the rape?"

"Yes. Her panties."

Something to remember. Stash it. Relive the thrill.

Ursa must not bring women home. If one nosy broad were to open his closet door while he was in the shower or fixing a midnight snack, she'd lose her marbles. Just looking for a man's T-shirt to wear to bed, the afterglow of sex still intoxicating, and then seeing rape trophies on display. He'd kill her. If he wasn't planning on it anyways. He'd have to.

On the right hand wall of my wife's closet there are some of her trinkets. Her elephant collection, some photographs. Her last pack of gum. Her lotion. My mouth fills with the ghostly taste of her after she'd chew that damned peppermint gum. Her favorite. Or how her skin was always a mixture of coconut and ginger. The softness of her lips. Her exhales along my cheek.

Ursa has a single shelf, a short piece of unattractive wood. On top of it, trinkets. A mishmash of bizarre items, probably taken in a fleeting moment of opportunity where he'd have to steal what was in front of him or nothing at all. A piece of costume jewelry. A wooden clothespin. A hair tie. The pink ceramic elephant I made my wife in my junior year art class.

Every electronic I can get torn from their cords and wires and dropped in the tub.

Stopper in the drain. Water turned on, slow. Knife to his space foam mattress. Gutted like it was a soldier standing next to a Bouncing Betty. Closet door torn off the hinges. Fat Sharpie marker drawing arrows along the wall to lead the authorities to the closet. And just because I'm a furious juvenile, I also draw huge dicks everywhere. Spurting and numerous, up and down the walls.

I check thoroughly through all his drawers and cabinets for other things of my wife's. I tear through his hallway closet, his clothes. Dump out every container in his kitchen. Root through his fridge; pull up his carpet in huge tears. Turn over the furniture. Cut open pillows and cushions. Smash glasses and plates. I don't find anything else.

Sit down at his computer and surf his bookmarks. Find his bank account. He's auto-saved his login information and I open his account. He's only got three thousand dollars in the bank. He must still have thousands from the blackmailing money somewhere else. Cash. I take his information to a toy store's website. Order three grand in dolls. Guy dolls. Rush delivery.

Yank the computer out. Drop it in the tub.

Search the sides of his mattress, find a slit. I pull it apart; see wads of money right next to a cigar box. Grab the money, count it. Not nearly enough to add up to what he's blackmailed. The cigar box. Grab it. Drop it on the bed. Burnt spoon, a package of needles a diabetic can buy for a few bucks at the corner drug store. A wad of heroin in a baggie. Cotton balls and sterile water. It's all coming together now. He's used the money to feed his addiction. So simple.

I pocket the money. Ursa doesn't need it and Petticoat isn't going to pay me now.

Take Ursa's cordless phone in hand and before I leave I dial a number.

"Vincenti's Pizza, home of the Taste Bud Burster, will this be delivery or carry-out?"

"Delivery."

"Okay, what can I get for you?"

"Anchovie Taste Bud Burster. And put one of your dessert pizzas on it. Not separate. *On* it."

"Seriously."

"Seriously. I'm crazy like that."

"Okay. What else?"

"That's it."

"May I have your telephone number?"

"No."

"Well...I need to get that and an email address, so—"

"Just deliver it here and tell the driver I tip well." I give him the address and hang up. Phone goes in the tub.

I leave, apartment door open. Elephant in my pocket, going back to my place to put it back with its friends. Then I will find him and peel him apart for days.

For days.

36

"Hello, Dick," his slithering queer says.

I whip the car into a parking lot. Some frozen yogurt hole in the wall. A neon clown waves at me from the window and the image is not lost on me.

"How have you been?" I ask, smiling. "Healing well?"

"I have been a busy bee, Dick. A busy, *busy* bee."

"You don't say? Come home yet?" The elephant in my palm, turning slowly.

"I've been to a few homes, yes."

"Boyfriends? Scared to sleep alone at night now?"

"So funny, Dick. I remember you sleeping—"

"Let's finish this. You and me. Name the place."

"So high school freshman of you, Dick. I bet the cheerleaders loved you."

"Of course they did. Have you seen me? When I came around, those girls ovulated and couldn't concentrate on anything else." He coughs a horse laugh at that. "But I bet all the KY in the world wouldn't help them when you came prowling. You seem to have that effect, Ursa."

"Ahhh...so we are on a first name basis, now."

"Indeed. Back to my original proposal. Let's finish this."

"I have another idea I'd like to bounce off of you: I'm gone."

"Well, first impression is you're a big smelly pussy."

"Sticks and stones, Dick. My childhood in Saint Ansgar was

vile, to say the least. You try staying in a town where your mom committed suicide on your first birthday and your dad spent his days putting out his cigarettes on your stomach and his nights getting drunk and making you take her place. You have no earthly fucking clue. I'm done."

"So you had a bad childhood. Get in line. Does that give you carte blanche to rape women?"

"You'll never understand."

"Don't care. This is all too little, too late. You're a fucking rapist and murderer. Your life is forfeit. I tell you what; meet me and I will make it swift and painless. Release you from this horrible life."

"This is a courtesy call to let you know you'll never see me again."

"Ursa, when you attack a woman, do you fantasize that she is your mother?" Silence. So much silence, heavy as the sun's gravitational pull. "Your mother, the woman who chose suicide over you? Who killed herself on your birthday and allowed you to be molested and—"

"Goodbye, Dick."

"*I'll find you. You know that, right?*"

"It's not my fault, Dick. It's how I was made." Click.

No caller ID. I hang up. I have the urge to walk over to that neon clown and slug him. It's a nice fantasy and I entertain it for a moment before my phone rings again, bursting that bubble like a drain backing up.

"Glad you called back, pussy. Reconsider?" I ask.

"Rrr—Richard?" Graham says through molasses. "I—I thought this was...this was...9-1..."

"Graham? Graham what's wrong?"

I have been a busy bee, Dick. A busy, busy bee.

I hear Graham's dog mewl in the background.

I've been to a few homes, yes.

37

My brakes screech to a halt and all I see are emergency vehicles.

Two black and whites aimed at Graham's house like their grills were going to zero in and open fire; driver side doors left wide open. An ambulance waiting off to the side, the crew poised at the rear of their truck, waiting for the all-clear.

"Whoa, mister, this is—" one of the medics says as I step out of my car and approach the house.

"Crime scene. I know. I called it in. This is my old partner's house. I'm former Saint Ansgar PD. What's the status? There should be a man and woman in there. What—"

"Okay. Okay. Just wait until the police clear it and we can go—"

I draw my .44 and the crew all stare like I pulled out my junk and flopped it on a nun's desk. I look at the lone female, say, "Honey, you're gawking at this like it's the first time you've laid eyes on nine inches."

"Your wife is kind if she told you that's what nine inches looks like."

I turn to the house and start walking. "I'm told this is nine inches, you're told you're pretty. Same difference."

No response to that. "Have the cops brought out anyone? Anyone at all?"

"Mister, if we had a patient we'd be working on them."

I look back to the house. The crime scene is cold. Ursa is

long gone. The cops inside must be clearing it and wasting valuable seconds. I wave the gun. "We're going in."

They follow.

"Police! Coming in with EMS!" I shout through the front door. Graham is on the living room carpet. Face down. Cell phone still in his hand. Blood caked to the side of his head. Jumped. Motherfucker. Clocked over the noggin and now—

"Show me your hands!" A uniform comes around the corner, sees me among the EMS. They move away from me and tend to Graham. EMS are crazy. The things they ignore to do what they do.

I hold my hands up, ID in one and the gun in the other.

The EMS chick looks to the uniform, says, "Jenkins, right? This dude claims to be PD. Came in with us."

One of the EMS guys says over his shoulder, "Said he was the RP."

The uniform comes over, takes my ID. Retired PD credentials. Examines them, takes a deep breath and holsters. Gives me the ID.

"You found the woman?"

The uniform raises an eyebrow. "You need to get out to the driveway and wait. We've got this."

Oh, if this kid worked for me back in the day. "I asked you a question, rookie. Where is this man's wife?"

"I don't know, now get the fuck outta our crime scene and wait like any other RP at the end of the drive."

EMS stabilizes Graham's neck and rolls him onto his back, onto a spine board. His phone slips out of his hand. The female picks it up and I snap, flex open and close my hand. She slaps it in my palm with enough attitude to turn me on if this were any other crime scene. Graham groans and tries to move. EMS holds him down. His eyes flutter, his lips curl like he's going to vomit. Or cry Molly's name.

I lean in. "Graham, it's Richard. I. Will. Find. Molly. *Alive.* I swear it to you."

He clears his throat. "You...have to."

"I will."

"The b—box..." he weakly motions to the mail organizer/key hook which adorns the wall next to the front door.

I look; see two pegs but only one set of keys. Two handcuff keys strung on the ring. Graham's then. Graham's unmarked car is out in the driveway. Molly's car, the shitbox as we call it, is not.

I nod, leave.

I light up a smoke as I cross through the front door, take the steps in one drop and hit the grass. I work Graham's phone and find the cell phone locator app he has installed on it. Molly's phone comes up, a flashing dot superimposed on a map. The street is labeled; nine blocks north and three to the west.

Got the location, got the getaway car. I walk past the black and white with its door standing wide open, flick my cigarette inside. Hopefully it's that rookie cocksucker who thinks I'm any old reporting party waiting for him at the end of the drive.

"Sorry, pencil dick. I've got someplace to be." And I roll out. Nine blocks to the north and three to the west.

38

The first time I saw Molly, I thought of classic Hollywood.

The way her hair seemed to glow in the sunlight like a halo. My wife's did that. No one else's did until Graham introduced me to his bride. Her big smile, capped under high cheekbones. Molly wore her eye shadow in a complete circle around her eyes, which set them off as a sparkling, dazzling electric blue.

"Richard, this is Molly. She's the one who liked the Oktoberfest brew over the autumn lager," Graham said as he motioned to her, quaintly dressed in gray plaid with red lips.

We were waiting outside a steakhouse so I could catch a smoke before we were seated. He had been bugging me to meet his wife for months and I had kept putting it off because Denise in Records said she'd seen Molly and thought Molly was a whale who fancied herself a whore.

Couldn't be further from the truth. I should have known; Denise herself needs to buy two airplane tickets and gets easily threatened by any woman who isn't dead. Women are so catty.

"Don't marry her then," I said, extending a hand to shake hers. "The Oktoberfest was swill compared to the lagers."

Graham and I had been drinking the local brewery's stuff a lot around that time. I knew Graham had been dating Molly since before he'd become a cop and they were married shortly after he graduated the academy, which was great for their honeymoon.

"I see why Graham has kept you hidden from me for so long, Richard," Molly said, shaking my hand.

"Why's that?"

"Because I punch anyone who drinks that autumn lager."

"You beat your husband?"

"He drinks Oktoberfest at home with me. I think he's humoring you with that lager."

I gave Graham a sidelong glance. He shrugged, turned red.

"Sonofabitch, Graham," I said. "Your wife is going to punch me and you've been lying about beer? This whole time?"

Graham put an arm around Molly and said, "I think our table is ready."

I never invited him for an autumn lager again. I don't booze with liars.

Reaching back to those memories, how her strawberry perfume mingled with my rib dinner that night, I think to how Graham would never say anything without bringing his wife into the conversation. How they never had children. How they almost adopted twice before being nitpicked and rejected at the last minute. Once I saw her looking at a professional picture of all these happy, chubby babies lined up and smiling, and her hand absently caressed her own womb. Found nothing. How Graham told me she had four brothers and two sisters.

But she was happy. She was fulfilled. A good man loved her and now she's stuffed in her own car and if I don't do something right now, she's as good as morgue-bound.

I check the blinking dot on the phone and gun it harder.

Hardware store.

The shitbox is parked out in BFE, near the exit to the road. I roll up and leave my own car running, charge up to the driver's side and see it's empty. Molly's cellphone is in the cup holder where she leaves it all the time. She also has a bad habit of leaving the window rolled down and therefore has a bad record of said cell phone getting stolen right out of her car.

The rapist has left it unrolled as well. I lean in, pop the trunk. A muffled scream. I come around the car and she's bound but flailing about, trying to kick in the face whoever walks up.

"Good girl," I say and dodge a blow. Lean in; lift her out with an arm. Shut the lid. Pocketknife cuts her gag and wrist bindings. She starts bawling and wraps her arms around my throat. I squeeze her tight and watch the hardware store's front entrance. No skeezy perv coming out.

I grab her face, tilt it up to me. No blood, swelling or otherwise. Eyes puffy from crying. Edges of her mouth rubbed raw from the gag. I look her up and down. Squeeze her shoulders, rotate her arms in my hands, pat her hips. She bears her own weight.

"Move quick, Molly. Quick."

"Richard! Richard! That guy! He's beat up and he's so high—I think—"

"I know, I know. Round two is coming right up."

I kneel, cut her ankle bindings. Stand. Even with her stark, red eyes and the way the terror of the past few minutes have stained her, have bled upwards and out through her skin like grease, she is gorgeous. And alive.

"Richard! He's inside! He's—" but her voice distorts with the first runner of color across my vision. Not again. Not again.

"Not again." I grumble. "Smear."

"Richard! No! You've got to—"

"Quiet. Get out. Call PD. Go. Go!" I push her away and she stares at me for a second and I turn away. My car is eight stalls down. "Go!" I shout over my shoulder and stumble towards it. Get in. Got to. Just get in—

I look back. Molly is beating feet through the intersection. A car honks but she keeps on keepin' on. Makes it to a grocery store.

Six stalls and the deluge begins. Purples squiggle and make

noise. They give way to a calming pink and I get four stalls away. Some old lady gives me the bug eyes as I lumber past her, dragging each foot and my lips wet with drool.

Two stalls and my left eye goes cold and blank. I risk it and try to run. Zombie shuffle. Hand on my door handle and I feel it bulge up in my guts. Knees weak. Colors start to run down my brain, freezing everything as they come. Door open. Head inside and the world falls away in a gorgeous waterfall of everything in my mind being dumped out into my lap.

39

The world falls back into place one starkly distinct pixel at a time; a puzzle piece falling light as snow until it collects to my head and fills in another missing bit of me.

Each cuts like an icepick through my forehead and my eyes feel like they've swollen twice their size. My knees burn and I can feel a breeze travel up my thighs. I peel my face off the pleather driver's seat and find that I went black, dropped to my knees on the parking lot and hit the seat face first.

Tore the knees out of my pants. No cops, no medics called to a check the welfare in the parking lot. Armed man passed out in his car. Thank God for the little things.

I pull myself up; see where I pissed my pants. Taste bile. Look over eight stalls. No shitbox. I lean my head back, ease a smoke into my mouth. A cop car cruises by on the street, turns into the grocery. Molly.

Fresh kidnappings give you a tiny window of action before the trail shits the bed. Sure, the bad guy may send a ransom note or whatever, but unless he wants to exchange the victim for money, you're looking at someone's life clock winding down. For about twenty minutes that was Molly.

Better to not dwell on all the rape/murder victim images flooding my mind. Stop putting my best friend's wife's face on all their bodies.

I feel self-satisfied that I trashed old boy's apartment and beat the fuck out of him. Took away his haunts, his resources. He wanted vengeance, but needed it on the fly. This hardware stop...I can't imagine what he bought.

But then I look down to Graham's cellphone and see a little dot blinking, superimposed on a map as it travels south. Nineteen blocks deep so far and counting.

My money is on that he doesn't know Molly is gone. But he might. In the end it doesn't matter. Maybe I'll go find out what he bought. And then use it on him.

40

Three-story construction in the ghetto, all flat concrete walls and unfinished rebar.

No windows, doors. Nothing permanent. Just boards hastily nailed into place. In the lot next to it is a sister construction. Just as unfinished and left to rot in the world. Molly's shitbox blends in with the neighborhood. The trunk is left standing open, as if the rapist left it that way so his little dove might return when it sees how inviting that cavern is.

And in this neighborhood, locked in a truck might be the safest place.

The dirt under the rear end is scrambled and torn up like he was standing there as a hive of bees attacked. Footprints and ruts in the soil where his heels dug in, swirls and scrapes like he was dancing for his life. Must have been when he flung open the trunk and found her missing. Just lost his shit right then and there. Tantrum the likes of which nobody this side of Honey Boo-boo has seen. Like Keith Moon and Stephen Dorff had a lovechild and set it loose in a hotel room. That kind of mess.

The taillights bashed in. The bottom lip of trunk lid looks like he found some way to slam it open and shut without it locking on him every time. The tire jack must be comfortably resting on the front seat since it appears he threw it through the back window.

Cry baby.

I cruise by, park a few blocks over. Hotfoot it to the construction. Ease out my iron; lead the way with the business end. I sneak inside as the sun sets to my left. As I hit each landing I spend some time looking across to the other construction; telltale signs that he's got a camp in there somewhere.

Here and there I kick a loose nail, crunch crumbled drywall. I duck and tread lightly but I still knock a wayward wrench off of a hip-level landing. It pings and settles; deafening as a firing squad. I crouch, wait for gunfire or the shadows to move. Something. But nothing comes.

Second floor. Only the wind rustling through to keep me on my toes. Nothing on the other side. Gang graffiti. Hobo trash. I skirt a long-deserted campfire on the floor and reach the third landing. A petroleum stink wafts down to me in little gulps, like the room is quietly belching fuel. I climb anyways. At the top is a window frame. I look long at the opposing building. Nothing but a good view of the roof of Molly's car.

The wall coming up the landing turns a corner behind me and I clear it in increments. Slicing the pie, the Tac guys call it. Little steps, gradually opening the room to yourself. Gun out, holding my breath. A wall of cardboard boxes gets in my way before I see much of anything. But I hear snoring.

Rapist? Bum? He parked next to that building and comes up here? Decoy? Throwing off the scent? Clever? Fuck it. Let's burn this place to the ground. Satisfaction rushes and my guts buzz with excitement. Motherfucker walks in on me while I'm wiped out and now I get to do it to him and—

Foot catches on a trip wire and as my body weight hitches forward, I think I smell the gasoline before it ignites.

The wire is across my shoe's tongue and I jerk and feel my knee pop something bad and my nose hits the concrete floor something worse and I must break a knuckle in my thumb cushioning my revolver as it hits the concrete something awful and the Universe is laughing at me about how this piece of shit is always one step ahead and then—

God intervenes. The trip wire is hung up on my shoe, but nothing has blown.

Silence. Keep it silent. See if the snoring skips or adjusts. Stops, maybe. I lay in the quiet with my broken-thumb revolver aimed at the boxes. Life ticks away from us. Whoever is over there. If it turns out to be a homeless man sleeping one off I'm going to beat him to death and then carry him over to the other building, find the rapist and use the bum's corpse to beat him to death. I swear.

Absolute calm licks at the walls and the sun draws its scalp down below the horizon.

Palms on the ground. Push up gently. Ease the tension on the wire. The faucet of my busted nose splatters on the concrete. I rest an arm under it so my jacket absorbs the crimson. Thumb throbs, holding my breath burns. I need a smoke. This takes time. I risk getting my flashlight from my pocket, fire it up against the wall behind me. Draw the beam until it catches the silk thread of the trip wire.

Follow it. Follow it. One end tied around a pipe stub-up. Next to it is a five-gallon can of gasoline. Why would there be a can of gas here, now? Don't know. Why do some women think that nineteen cats are a suitable replacement for a man? That I do know.

But the other end of the trip wire goes straight into a home-made bomb, pulled over on its side by me. Yanked it over in the fall. Holy shit, I'm not sprayed across the wall because whoever rigged this thing didn't anchor it the way it needed to be?

And everybody thinks God hates me.

I shrug the trip wire off my foot, still gentle—my luck enjoys cornholing me. I ease up, zero in on the snoring and make sure there are no other booby traps as I clear the boxes. First I see two brand-new lengths of chain. A drill bit fatter than most dildos and a hand crank for it. No power tool. Close and personal. Duct tape and wood clamps. A receipt from the hardware store that has more than ten items listed on which I'm not readily seeing in the pile. Oh Molly. God doesn't hate you.

Now I see it. At the bottom of the list there is the red gas can. What was he planning on doing?

Lying there with a cooked spoon and used needle beside a flop-mattress is the sexual deviant I should have beaten to death in a women's shower room.

41

The rapist's snores are deeper than anything Confucius ever said.

He looks weak. Worn thin. His life was pedestaled very high just a little while ago, and those have since crumbled and left to oblivion. His clothes are dirty and stink of not being washed for days. His hair, mussed and oily. I got him good; his face is an ugly purple from bruising.

The spoon and needle look used before now. His escape. Pain management. Brown, wet cotton balls scattered like dirty snow in his private hell. Molly's keys sitting on the floor near him. They go in my pocket. I lean in; put my barrel an inch from his head, just above the ear.

Why is he here? Just squatting? His blackmail money spent on heroin? He can't go to any area hospital; they'll have to call the cops. He'd get tied back to it all. He must have wanted one last hurrah before blowing this popsicle stand forever. Tiding over here tonight.

Half the trigger pull is out and I stop. Let it go. Back up, step over the trip wire. Look at the explosive. Glass jar filled with a gasoline gel. Suspended in the gel are razors and ball bearings. Like tidbits of pineapple and orange floating in Aunt Annie's Christmas Jello mold. This is just the vicious version.

It's wrapped in duct tape, packing it tight. The trip wire was supposed to drag a match along a striking surface and ignite some metallic-looking powder, which is piled neatly onto a sheet of cigarette rolling paper sitting atop the gel. Hmmm...

An angel on one of my shoulders, a devil on the other, they usually quibble but right now they're putting their heads together. Then all of a sudden the angel is licking her lips and doing a little dance while the devil is twirling his greasy mustache between two fingers while a dastardly laugh escapes. I got it.

"Hey, douche, sleep tight until I come back," I say. Leave.

42

I come flying up to my favorite intersection, which just so happens to be seven blocks south and five west.

Baltimore and 42nd.

The Carnivore Messiah's new hooptie comes screeching out of the shadows and stops in my path. The same dickhead comes strolling out from under a porch awning and I get giddy with my luck. He's six feet from the car when I swing open my door.

The front and back passenger doors on the hooptie open, thugs pop out. The dickhead sees me and once my face clicks in his memory he shits his pants. Oh goodie. Wheels his hands in thin air. Backpedals. Stumbles, lands on his sweet little tush.

I rush forward, iron out. I put two through the hooptie's passenger side. Glass shatters. The thugs raise their guns. I drop one where he stands. The second one fires wildly and tries to take cover in front of the car.

The driver and some other dude hop out, come around with their pieces aimed in my general direction. Which, since they're gang members, doesn't mean much.

Dickhead scrambles away from me, a kind-of crabwalk as he scurries. His pants are belted just above his knees and dragging his ass along the street pulls them down around his ankles. "It's him!" he shouts and his voice squeaks with it. Nothing makes me more proud of my effect on people than when grown men screech like women as they announce my presence.

"It's fuckin' him! The guy that jumped us!"

I'm the guy that jumped a robbery set up? Of course I am.

The thugs hear that and they run. Don't bother with the car. Don't bother with revenge. Don't even bother with rescuing their dead homie or the living one right in front of me. They beat feet in the opposite direction.

I snag this fucker by the collar; lift him up. "That's gotta make you feel good, don't it?"

"W—what?"

"Your whole crew jets when I show up, and leave you here with me."

"What you want, man?"

"I want Thuggie."

"Nah, man. Nah. Kill me. I ain't no snitch and I—"

Uppercut to his guts and whatever he was going to finish that sentence with gets lost in the forced exhale. His feet leave the street and my knuckles rub along the interior of his spine. I let go of his collar. He hits the ground hard.

I go down to one knee beside him, dig through his pockets. Gasping, he squirms. Tries to get stupid. Now, I've punched a lot of people. Hitting them while they're standing up is best because you've got all that room behind their head to snap back. When you drill someone lying down—especially on concrete—the give ain't what it is when they're upright. The plus side they get hit twice. The downside is I've broken my hand more times than I can count. Oh well.

I drill him.

The concrete hits the back of his head as hard as I hit his jaw and lights out.

Find his cellphone in a pocket and pull it out. Some weed and rolling papers fall out as well. A condom. Some pocket change. This guy must have had only one pocket he trusts. Scroll through the phone—which is a cheap piece of shit, by the way—find Thug Dawg. Winner winner chicken dinner. Dial the number.

One eye on the phone, one eye on the punk before me. He stirs just a bit. Blinks a bunch. Groans and one hand rubs his face. He probably doesn't think it, but I see him reaching behind his back.

"What?" Answers the phone.

"Thuggie?"

"'Course! Man, what the fuck is going—"

"Thuggie, you must think I'm the turd whose name is on your caller ID. I'm the guy who rolled your Baltimore and Forty-second intersection crew. Burned down your cathedral. Know me?"

A moment of recognition and I can hear him draw in a furious breath. "Mother fucka, you ain't got no idea how bad it's gonna be when—"

"Yeah, yeah. I don't think you have the hair on your balls to come get me yourself. I don't think you've got 'em."

"You don't? For real? Are you playin'?"

"Nope. I hear you're too big of a bitch to do the work yourself 'cuz you're afraid of sucking more dick inside prison. Am I right?"

"Oh...oh you're goin' die slow 'cuz of that. Slow."

"Liar liar pants on fire."

"Put Jamoneon back on. We're gonna make some arrangements—"

"Is Jamone the guy quivering on the ground in front of me?"

Jamone hears that and makes his move. He starts to swing a gun around from his lower back—a tiny thing I should have found in the search. Damn you, Richard, stupid, stupid—and I plug one round through him. He drops, the gun clattering to the road.

"Correction, *was* Jamone the guy quivering on the ground in front of me?"

"I will fuckin' kill you! I will—"

"You and whoever you wanna bring, meet me at the corner of Parker Avenue and Thirty-fifth Terrace. Twenty minutes.

You got me? Twenty minutes or I tell the world how you pussed out and how easy I'm rollin' up on your turf. When you get there call this number."

"Mother fu—"

Click.

Back in the car. Gone.

43

Back to the construction site and I park behind some pile of debris, see that Molly's shitbox is still there.

Can't roll up the window. I grab her phone, stash in it my jacket. Pull out Molly's keys and move the vehicle up the block and into the parking lot of a church. Hotfoot it back. I hit the building and take the stairs two at a time until I reach the third floor landing. Stop. Listen for that wonderful snoring again. Still there. I cut the trip wire. Move a wooden crate about waist-high over by the window that has an unobstructed view out to the other building. Put two cardboard boxes on it. Inside one box I put the explosive.

Pull out my knife, grab the gasoline jug. Cut the whole top off.

The rapist wakes up when I throw the entire jug on him.

"Ahhhh!" he jumps up, starts jiggling and writhing like he was fighting for the lead role in *Flashdance*.

I close the gap, swing a right hook so hard he spins in a pirouette and a loose tooth flies out, hits the wall. He drops, rolls around cradling his jaw.

"I got the girl."

He nods as much as one can while their face is cracked. Coughs. Wipes at his face as the gasoline stench clears my nostrils.

He spits on me. Snarls. "If they didn't want it they should

have fought harder," he says. Vindictive. He wants to cry. I can see it, but he won't give me the satisfaction. He tears off his shirt, uses his forearms to scrub at his face.

"Just smearing it around, home boy," I say.

He coughs so hard it triggers his gag reflex. Gets one eye open enough to look at me. "Men like you...and bitches. If bitches earned...the things they have it would've been— would've been them who...conquered nations and built build- ings and—and—and created reading and writing and diverted rivers. But fuck no. Fuck no! They want to be...*equal* to men without being equal. I'm—I'm no twat's fucking equal and if if if...some chick looks at me like she's better than me she's gonna—she's gonna fuckin' learn she ain't!"

"Said every pussy ever." I circle him like a lion around prey. "I was married once, and I put her on a pedestal. Not because she could lift as much weight as me, but because she was everything I was not, and that made me want to lift the weights for her."

"So Goliath has his inner teddy bear." Coughs, hacks up whatever bile is in his stomach. "Go fuck yourself."

"Actually," I say, leaning back against a wall, "this ends here. And that leads me to my next point. I would lift all the burdens in the world for my wife, but you, you're gonna have to do it yourself."

"They'll never take me alive."

"I know. Which is why you're soaked in gasoline." I produce a matchbook. Drop it next to him. "So get it going."

"Get what going?"

"Your exit."

"Are you outta your fuckin' mind?"

"Nope." I light a smoke. "Right now, some gangbangers I know are on their way over here. Remember this necklace?" I show him the pearls he stole from me. "These rightfully belong to the aunt of the gang's head honcho. The big cheese. And he's gonna be pissed when he finds them in your possession."

"I'll dime you out in a heartbeat."

I casually stroll over. He braces as he sees the lit cigarette in my right hand. Never sees the left hook coming.

I back up. Take a drag. "You won't be diming out anybody with that broken mouth."

He's on his back rolling around, his entire jaw in pieces, held as shards inside his skin. Sounds like he's choking but I bet it's only another tooth. He hacks and gags, clears his airway.

"Your deviance has led you here. Your thirst for hurting others has led you here. Your filth has led you here. And now, I'm making sure it gets stomped out. I didn't ask you to butcher the lives of so many helpless people. So light the match before they get here."

He just rolls, lays on his side.

I kneel down, whisper, "You've heard of the Carnivore Messiahs? You've heard of their rivals? How they die? They rape men, you know. Prison justice. They do things that would make BTK poop his britches. And for a serial killer who took his time with children, that's saying something."

I stand, walk away. Turn my back as I near the stairs. "Leave the matches alone, I don't care. Take your chances."

I hear him, ever so slightly, inch against his conscience across the floor. The slide of wet fabric across concrete. Trepidatious fingers, scrawling gasoline swirls and lines until those fingertips touch the matchbook. He starts to cry, and all I hear are the whimpers and pleadings of so many women under his bulk, their underwear being torn at until they rest limp around their ankles. Tears wetting their bloody cheeks. Finding that far-off place where they can be away from what's happening.

All I hear is Petticoat's wife as she beseeches her unconscious husband to defend her. All I hear is Molly trying to scratch her way through the trunk lid, wanting to know why Graham actually went down when he was bashed over the head. All I hear is the muffled voices of however many other women this guy has destroyed throughout his hideous career.

Then I hear the match head flare up, *whoosh,* and heat play against my back. I hear screaming. Real screaming. Accepting his fate but not the agony of it, apparently. I count to five and pick up the bucket of water I brought with me, turn around and throw it on him.

The flames hiss and go back to hell, sizzling out to nothing and the rapist is here with me, lobster red and every nerve exposed.

But alive.

I think back to Willibald's WWII story about the French woman. *I remember how she just grasped her groin and moaned like she had been set on fire for a minute and put out. Left to suffer until Death swooped in with its talons. Just never came. Not that way, anyhow.*

"Death is coming, perv," I say, rolling my head on my shoulders. "Death is coming."

44

"Bye, Ursa. They'll be here soon."

And I roll down the stairs, leave his squeaking mewls up on the third floor. I hit the second landing and the phone rings.

I look out a window, see three ghetto sleds roll up; queefs pile out like they were clowns in the center ring. "Yo, Thuggie?"

One guy stalks around like he owns the place. All the others give him a wide birth but circle him like he was radiating their source of power. "Where you at, mother fucka? I'ma get my hands on you—"

"Right here, sexy boy." And I fire four rounds. The night comes to life with sparks as I shoot to piss them off.

They drop and swing their barrels up and around, looking for something to zero in on. I give them the other two rounds, leaving a muzzle flash in the night sky.

They see it, send lead my way. Good girls. I duck, find the first floor as quiet as a two hundred sixty pound mouse. Tiptoe out a window, barrel across the space between the two buildings in a wide arc. While they're staring at the empty air near the muzzle flash I'm entering the next house.

I hit a room, brace against a wall and pop my cylinder. Reload. Go up the stairs. Keep it low, scan the shadows until I see them again, racing around across the way, their silhouettes darker against a dark background inside. Heads bobbing as

215

their idiotic, blind rage takes them up the stairs in a manner that makes me yearn to be at the top with a machine gun. This is what fish in a barrel look like.

Tactics out the window. Revenge's handicapped little brother has removed his safety helmet and taken the wheel. I see them pour onto the second floor and I bide my time while they search and toss over every shadow and dust mote looking for that guy who jumped their crew.

And then, the rapist's pathetic mewling must catch their ears. I hear them explode in acknowledgements; "There's that moutha fucka!" "Upstairs! Go! Go!" "Cap his ass!"

Head on up, fellas. And they do. Nuts to butts they charge up there, spilling onto the third floor. I see the last guy nearly trip over himself getting up there, zooming around. I think about Ursa, about all those times he called me Dick. If there's one thing I insist upon, it's that no one calls me Dick. No one.

I take a deep breath and put the front sight on the box with the gel explosive in it. Squeeze, squeeze, squeeze. Surprise.

My barrel barks into the still night and the third floor comes alive with all the fury of the sun.

45

Orange roils outward, the shade of a tiger after you stab him in the ass.

Boiling, the explosion is red at the edges like what any man sees as he enters his bedroom to find his wife occupying another man's time. Black curls in as the first real precursors of death. The fat burst rises and sweeps in under itself; bulging out into a bulb. Rising on a column of flame. Mushroom.

The building around me snaps to life with peppered debris. Concrete slabs and pebbles, no doubt razor blades and ball bearings as well. I duck, feel a rain of dirt and rubble sprinkle down on me for long, long seconds.

I wait until I hear the quiet susurration of hissing flame, of ruins settling down into piles. Then I look up. Where the third floor was, there is now a black char mark. The outer walls are jagged teeth of blasted wreckage. Smoke billowing. Holes in the floor, pocked about like acne in all its varying degrees of severity. No rapist. No gang.

I stand up.

Something crunches behind me and I feel the gunshot before I hear it. My breath leaves in a great whoosh as powerful as that explosion and my face hits the window frame. Down. Guts on fire. Feel a fist grab me around the ankle and yank me back. Taste the concrete as it slides across my teeth.

Try and roll, try and struggle. Futile. Every organ I have just quivers and has teeth, chewing at my insides. Vision blurs and gets grainy. If I can just stand up, if I can just make a fist. But in the end my spine just quits bending and my hands quit clenching and my will to stop acting like a flopping fish on the shoreline evaporates. I'll just rest a second. Get my second wind.

A fire has started in the back of my ribs, left side. Maybe right. Can't tell anymore. Hard to breathe.

Footsteps around me. Shoes sliding along the bare concrete, shuffle shuffle shuffle. Whoever it is they need to pick up their feet when they walk. Kick to help me roll over on my back. Someone else's hand in my jacket, taking my iron. Kicked once, twice in the face. Before my eye swells shut I see Thuggie standing over me.

46

"This is it, mother fucka. This is where your war led you."

"Thuggie..." that name slides off my tongue the way a stomach rejects rotten food. The night of Willibald's death comes rushing back, bulldozing. *I see his face just enough to feel secure in the fact that the next time I see it'll be beating to death the right coward. The facial hair, the baby cheeks and high eyebrows. Ugly.*

"I recognize you. Pussy," I say. "Always shooting when your target isn't ready."

He aims his piece down over my face. He looms there like the angel of death; gun metal gray scythe with a four-inch barrel guiding the way. His foot on my chest and all I can think about is how baggie his fucking pants are. They pool around his ankle the way a dad's slacks do when his child tries them on for size.

"I ain't got no rules, pig. And I play the game to win."

"You got not balls, either."

I groan, arch my back. I can feel the slug shift in my ribs. I scream. The agony of that little critter burrowing. My toes curl and as stupid as it sounds that tiny sensation puts life in my blood. The bullet, shallow and low. Missed my spine. My heart. I feel it throb through my neck, flooding my brain. My lungs burn but no pressure is building. They're intact.

"War?" I ask through gritted teeth. "How 'bout your fucking foot soldiers shoot up the right house? *This* is where your war led to."

"Fuck that old lady." His tone is flat. The life of a woman wasted means literally nothing.

I spit some blood across his shoe. "Tell me somethin', bro. Word on the street was...when you came back for—for the second drive-by, you. You were the shooter."

He gives me the cockiest half-smile this side of *Magnum P.I.* "Fuck that old geezer, too."

He points my own gun at me with his other hand, adjusts his grip, finger on the trigger. "Fuck you. I ain't never killed a cop before."

Shadows shift from across the room. I smell a change in the wind. I laugh. "I'm not a cop. But you will be killing the last swinging dick to make your mama slip around in her own goo."

"You funny. You very—" And Thuggie's head snaps forward. He pitches over against the wall behind me just as blood and brains start finding their way out of his mouth.

"You heard that?" I squeak out. The shadows shift again and Graham comes forward, looking like shit.

"The your mama joke?"

"No."

"The part about killing my grandfather?" Graham asks.

"Yup. You heard it."

I try to roll onto my side and the pain floods up. Nearly pass out.

"Stop. Stop." Graham's hands lay on and things come in snatches from there. I know I take my weapon back from Thuggie. Then darkness. We make it downstairs. I know that much. Next thing I remember is trying to ask how he found me.

He says something like his heart led me to him. Graham pats me down, pulls out Molly's cellphone. I see his laptop in the backseat. A little dot blinking on its screen. I lay my head against the window; pass out as we drive off.

Last thing I remember is him gunning it onto the highway and thanking God we missed the emergency responders.

47

At first I think Graham is talking to me, but when I look over he's on the phone.

"Yes, I can make that go away," he says, looking annoyed. "You do this for me, I do that for you."

Out the window and the highway is long gone. Blacktop has changed to gravel. Buildings to thickets of trees. The drone of insects has replaced the roar of engines. We hit a bump and the flare of pain in my back nearly puts me out again. My vision constricts and I want to vomit.

I hear Graham say, "Deal. I'm around the corner now."

I pass out as he turns down a driveway in the middle of nowhere.

Manhandled out of the car.

"You're not drunk right now, are you?" Graham asks. I want to say no, but another voice chimes in.

"Nah. Just a nip, just to take the edge off."

"What edge?" Graham asks. I can feel his hands under my armpits, carrying me. Someone else has my feet. Speaking of a drink, I need one. My head swims and I can't fight through the semi-unconscious fog.

"When a cop calls you in the middle of the night to sew up one of his buddies, I'm not stupid," that other voice says. Gruff.

Female. "I know this is some shady shit. I'm down; you're one of the good guys. But, you're lucky I need the money."

Graham huffs and nearly trips over a stick or something. My body jitters hard and I must cry out because Graham starts apologizing. Then I hear him say, "You need a charge fixed. *You're* lucky I need this."

"Yeah, yeah. All right, fine. Five hundred for parts and labor, fix the DUI. I take care of your friend. Deal?"

"Deal," Graham says.

I hear a door open and AC hits my skin. I feel a smooth, hard metal table underneath me and the other voice must be rummaging through some instruments on a tray. Someone tugs at my pant leg and the unmistakable sound of scissors cutting fabric fills the room. A straight line goes up my shin to my knee and the blunt scissors tip bumps the flesh of my kneecap. Moves on to my thigh.

"How do you fix the DUI, anyway?" the other voice asks. "You just wait 'til no one's looking and tear up a piece of paper? Something like that?"

"I wish," Graham says. "Who is this guy?"

"Hey. Name's Ian. Good to meet you."

I try and open my eyes enough to see just what in the hell is going on. I stir just enough to feel a hand firmly on my chest. Muscles are weak. My skin is getting tacky with the blood coming out of the bullet wound on my back. The voice belonging to this Ian fella speaks up, "Whoa, easy there, big guy. Let us work our magic."

Graham says, "What the hell is he doing here?"

The female says, "He's my tech. I need a second pair of hands when I'm operating on anything bigger than a Saint Bernard."

"Yeah, bro. It's cool," Ian says.

I try to stir again and that hand keeps firm pressure. "Whoa, easy there, big guy."

Graham says, "He's a man. Not a horse."

"It's cool. It's cool."

I feel a cold sensation in my elbow, then hear, "You're going to feel a little poke in one, two, three..."

The needle goes in. I catch a lungful of air and just go with it. As the world sinks away I hear Graham say, "I'm not paying your tech."

I want to tell him to not be so cheap, but I fade away as I feel them roll me to my side.

Two days later and I hobble down to the end of the driveway; wait for Graham to come pick me up.

I look out and see a herd of cattle across the way, grazing and generally not being bothered by the world. Somewhere I hear chickens. The breeze comes up over the rolling hills and splashes along my chest and back. I'm nude from the waist up, save the industrial-sized bandages wrapped around me.

"So anyway," Marla, the female vet who owns this place says. "Come back in two weeks and I'll take out the stitches. Beyond that, clean it with soap and water a few times a day. No physical activity besides the bare-minimum; getting in and out of bed and the car. Walking. No running. Try not to stretch while you yawn, reach for things above your head. You know the drill."

"Yeah, I know," I say, light up a smoke.

Marla sips from her morning eye opener, a bloody mary that I watched her prepare with two raw eggs and half a gallon of vodka, and she continues, "Quit smoking, if you get a fever or if the wound site starts leaking—"

I tune her out. Think about Carla Gabler. I need to go tell her things are squared away and Mickey can rest in peace. Marla, the DUI large animal vet and her idiot tech Ian patched me up. It's a double-edged sword going under the knife in someone's basement. If I show up to a hospital with a bullet in my back, the cops tend to ask questions. If I show up on someone's doorstep who needs a favor, well, that has its own risks. Fortunately, when Graham cut this deal with Marla, it was her first positive experience with the cops.

I see a rooster tail of gravel dust coming down the road and hope to God it's Graham. I want news about Molly's recovery, and I want a damn whiskey. I want a lot of whiskey.

This time Carla doesn't hesitate to open the door when I'm knocking.

"Hello, Richard. Come in. I have sweet tea." She smiles and seems to know I've come for the last time.

"Hi, Carla. Is Absinthe around?" I hold up a new doll I bought her. "It has a change of clothes that came right in the package with it, so I think it's pretty high falutin'."

Carla looks at the doll. "It is very pretty. Thank you."

"You're welcome." I look around, but no little girl.

"Her mom took her to a birthday party," Carla says. "I'm sorry. She'll be here tomorrow."

I fake a sad grimace and set the doll down on the table. "Well, nothing can stop her from playing with it tomorrow, eh?"

"Nope. Nothing." Carla lights a smoke and offers me a seat. Gets me a glass of tea. Sits down across from me. "Well, you're here for something. Spill it."

So I tell her. I never found out the details but Mickey is dead. She cries just a little and I let her. She needs it. I'm sure the bulk of those tears had come and gone years ago when she never saw him out of prison. I tell her the rapist died during apprehension and even though it's not a slow, agonizing death, Mickey's memory got its justice.

We blab on for a little bit, small talk. She recites a memory or two about her fallen love and I listen. She tells me about how Mickey was nice and sweet and likeable for all the months they were together. Apparently he wasn't one for bugs of any kind, and went out of his way to step on any that he saw.

"That was his cruel streak," Carla says. "I was always upset with him for how he would squash those little defenseless bugs. I don't know why it bothered me so. Maybe because it seemed sometimes that he was...I don't know, taking out his rage on them."

"Everyone has something," I say. "Was he phobic of some kind?"

"No. Just didn't like bugs."

"I see."

"His stepmother—Joann's birth mom—she got onto him about it all the time. Of course, by the time his dad and stepmom married both he and Joann were in their teens and Mickey I guess butted heads with her a lot. He missed his own mom."

"He did, huh?"

"Yes." Carla stood up. "Let me show you my favorite picture of us, okay?"

"Sure."

She goes to her closet—everyone keeps their treasures in a closet, I guess—and rummages through shoebox after shoebox. "We went on our one vacation together to Las Vegas. It was magical. All the lights and the sights and sounds. You could walk down the Strip at two in the morning and it would be alive with people and going-ons. The food was magnificent and it never ended. But anyways, we drove out to Hoover Dam and some kind stranger offered to take our picture."

She rummages some more, flipping through stack after stack. "No...no...that was...uh, 2000, I think. No...no...here it is! My favorite!"

She stands up and proudly walks over, the magic of the moment, alive and living again with her truest love, Mickey Cantu, she trots over to me like a beaming model that knows she's a shoe-in for the crown at the pageant.

Carla sits so close to me the fabric of her shirt runs along my skin. She hands me the picture and she does look lovely. The Hoover Dam in full majesty behind them, pouring ocean after ocean into the world. Carla is young and fresh. She looks radiant, and the way she stands, the look on her face, she's by happenstance identical to a picture I've seen before.

She looks just like Ursa Hanchett's mother in the picture he had on his kitchen counter. Which makes sense, because the man next to her is the rapist I set on fire.

"So, Mickey and you, huh?" I ask, handing back the picture.

"Yes. Those days could have gone on forever," Carla says, admiring the photo with a love that is as unstained and pure as an infant. "I wish they had."

"Me too," I say and pat her hand. She smiles and I let her think I mean something else. Eventually she puts the photo away.

"So, I'm a little confused on a few things," I say, and even though I'm starting a new conversation I stand up to leave. "Mickey's birth mother...divorced? Died? Was never around?"

"She, ummmm...she suffered a lot. From things. Addiction. Probably some kind of mental illness. She ended her suffering."

Took her own life, fell to her own hand, ended her suffering. Committed suicide. *Messed that boy up for life when she killed herself on the boy's birthday. Yeah. Crazy bitch did it on purpose.*

"Ahhh...and Mickey's dad eventually remarried?"

"Well, I'm not sure his parents were ever technically married, but yes. Mickey never spoke much about it. I just pieced it all together."

"Ever give you his birth mother's name?"

"Oh yes. Exotic but really bizarre. Ursula Cantu."

This just got weird. But all the pieces are falling into place, even if I have to fill in the gaps.

I say my goodbyes, and true to my original promise, I only

tell Carla the good. I don't bring up that her one true love was a deeply disturbed man. I don't say his real name was probably Mickey Hanchett and that after his mother died he probably pranced around in her house coat and curlers and wanted the world to call him Ursa and that everybody did except his own father. Then his father remarried and it caused a fissure in his life that reverberated forever. I don't tell her I'm sure Ursa spent his teenage years in a miasma of self-identity crisis. He probably wasn't a cat burglar. He was a home invasion rapist and the only break he took was when he found Carla. Her presence must have quieted the demons in his head. All he needed to vent his urges was to step on bugs and he'd feel power over something.

I don't tell Carla that she knew her love during one of his good streaks and that he probably loved her to the extremes he did because she was a spitting image of his own mommy. That maybe while he got to know Petticoat in prison he heard rumors of how Petticoat slept with all those women inmates and while Petticoat was trying to buy good will with Ursa by telling him how he "took care" of Carla, what Ursa really heard was Petticoat slipped her the big one and the burglary/insurance fraud thing was just sweet revenge.

I tell Carla only the good.

48

"The sky is beautiful today, all of it, it's all beautiful."

Molly's head is tilted to the heavens above, where no doubt Willibald and Eustace Clevenger are, looking down on us. I stand there, my back aching from being on my feet for the whole funeral. We're outside again, same spot in the boneyard, same crowd no doubt wearing the same black clothing they wore last week when we interred Eustace. Same rent-a-preacher. Graham next to me, still needing a few more days for the laceration he took to the head when Ursa Hanchett jumped him. He looks at peace, though, and for that I am thankful. Eternally thankful.

One would never guess that Molly spent a half hour in her own trunk, tied and gagged. She still has the shitbox car. I'll never understand her.

"Yes, it is beautiful," Graham says. Puts an arm around her and tugs her head forward in his elbow. He kisses her forehead and they share a loving glance. Graham turns to me.

"Where's mine?" I ask, smile. Molly leans over and punches me in the chest.

We start to leave and Detective Collins, the SAPD homicide dick who worked both Eustace and Willibald's cases, comes over to us. "Hey, boss, good news."

Graham shakes his hand. So do I. "I love good news," Graham says.

"Well, you know last week we found LaTrell 'Thuggie' Williams shot dead, correct?"

We all nod and Collins continues. "Anyway, the gang unit made short work of announcing that to the world. We also found a bunch of his boys burned to death in a building nearby. Whatever it was they were doing, I'm afraid to ask. Playing with fire, I guess. But, skirmishes have broken out all over the city."

"Vying for Carnivore Messiah territory?" I ask.

"Yes. The Carnivores are all but done with. We'll see splinter groups and new crews pop up, but Thuggie's legacy will be forgotten next week."

Molly scrunches her eyebrows, asks, "So what's the good news?"

We all look at her like she just said we should start calling soccer "football." I look at Graham and let him answer. "A bunch of gangbangers are dying, and best of all the people responsible for Grandma and Grandpa's deaths are among them. That's the good news."

Molly just stares at him. "You guys and your coppiness."

We talk for a while longer and eventually Collins makes his goodbyes. Leaves.

"Let's go. First round is on me," Graham says.

"I'm not drinking Oktoberfest," I say. "Let's get that clear."

Graham looks over and smiles at me. "Man, I haven't thought about Oktoberfest beer in a long time. I used to love to love that stuff."

"I'll kill you," I say.

We get to the car and Graham stops, gives me his serious look. "Richard, thank you."

I pat him on the shoulder and nod. "I'm not good at that stuff, Graham. Never have been."

"I know. But you need to hear it."

"Heard it. You're welcome."

He smirks. "Okay. Fine. That's out of the way now."

"Yes. Now we can get to the booze," I say and Graham steps inside the car, scoots over to Molly.

Graham laughs and says, "Booze. That's all you care about, Richard."

I look inside the backseat, see my only true friend and his wife, look at the shadows of bruises on their faces, see where Graham's lip was split but healing, feel the burning hole in my back. Think of the elephant I took from Ursa's closet and set back amongst my wife's other things.

"Booze isn't all I care about," I say to myself. Get inside next to them and shut the door on the whole mess.

ACKNOWLEDGMENTS

This book was a stop-and-go process that took me years to complete. I started writing it while my wife was pregnant with our third child. Now he's four as I'm typing all the not-story stuff that each book requires. Hell, child number five will be born before this book is actually published.

Benoit Lelievre deserves a special shout-out here. He runs the Dead End Follies website and reviews things—books, movies, the NBA, whatever else pops in there—as a second job. He took time out to read an earlier version of this (while still consuming books to review, writing his own stuff, working his day job and being the best dog owner he could be) and his comments made it a much stronger book. So, thank you Ben.

Susie Henry also deserves a special shout-out here. She's an astronaut or something, as well as a poet, photographer, editor, devoted mother and wonderful friend. She's been a huge supporter of my work since I met her and has informed me she would marry Buckner if he were real. She also took time out of her busy life to read an earlier version of this and her comments were fantastic. They dug at the nuanced stuff; stuff I never would have caught on a self-editing run. Her comments made it a much stronger book.

Chris Leek deserves a special shout-out here. My English brother from another mother, a much stronger writer than I'll ever be, and tall. He dug in deep here and I can't remember the shape the story was in before he came through and fixed it. What can I say? Chris mother fuckin' Leek, ladies and gentlemen. His comments made it a much stronger book.

And here is my standard disclaimer: I always wanted the book tuned slightly higher than reality—maybe up to 110%, because normal anything isn't entertaining enough—and I felt comfortable where I landed. It's exaggerated here and there. Mainly the violence. Whatever is written correctly, I was advised on. Whatever wouldn't fly in real life is squarely because of me.

ABOUT THE AUTHOR

RYAN SAYLES has over two dozen short stories in print, anthologies and online, including the Anthony-nominated collection *Trouble in the Heartland: stories inspired by the music of Bruce Springsteen.* He is the author of *Subtle Art of Brutality, Warpath, Goldfinches* and *That Escalated Quickly!* He is a founding member of Zelmer Pulp. He was in the military and is currently a police officer.

He's online at https://vitriolandbarbies.wordpress.com/.